YOUR recipe could appear in our next cookbook!

W9-CSQ-099

Share your tried & true family favorites with us instantly at

www.gooseberrypatch.com

If you'd rather jot 'em down by hand, just mail this form to...

Gooseberry Patch • Cookbooks – Call for Recipes
PO Box 812 • Columbus, OH 43216-0812

If your recipe is selected for a book, you'll receive a FREE copy!

Please share only your original recipes or those that you have made your own over the years.

Recipe Name:

Number of Servings:

Any fond memories about this recipe? Special touches you like to add
or handy shortcuts?

Ingredients (include specific measurements):

Instructions (continue on back if needed):

Special Code: **cookbookspage**

Over ➤

Extra space for recipe if needed:

Tell us about yourself...

Your complete contact information is needed so that we can send you your FREE cookbook, if your recipe is published. Phone numbers and email addresses are kept private and will only be used if we have questions about your recipe.

Name:

Address:

City: State: Zip:

Email:

Daytime Phone:

Thank you! Vickie & Jo Ann

Christmas Comfort Classics

A festive collection of warm and cozy comfort foods,
plus sweet ideas for sharing with family & friends.

Gooseberry Patch

An imprint of Globe Pequot
246 Goose Lane
Guilford, CT 06437

www.gooseberrypatch.com
1•800•854•6673

Do you have a tried & true recipe...

tip, craft or memory that you'd like to see featured in
a **Gooseberry Patch** cookbook? Visit our website at
www.gooseberrypatch.com and follow the
easy steps to submit your favorite family recipe.
Or send them to us at:

Gooseberry Patch
PO Box 812
Columbus, OH 43216-0812

Don't forget to include the number of servings your recipe makes,
plus your name, address, phone number and email address. If we
select your recipe, your name will appear right along with it...
and you'll receive a **FREE** copy of the book!

Contents

Dedication

To everyone who cherishes baking cookies, decorating the tree, singing carols and sitting down with loved ones to share the joy of Christmas over all the delicious dishes that make the holiday extra special.

Appreciation

To all of you who generously shared tried & true recipes for making the holidays bright...thank you, and a very merry Christmas!

Frosty Morning
Breakfasts

Red & Green Breakfast Egg Bake

Jodi Spires
Centerville, OH

The most delicious breakfast casserole that I have ever tasted...everyone who tries it agrees!

8-oz. tube refrigerated crescent rolls
1-1/2 lbs. ground pork breakfast sausage
2 T. butter
3/4 c. green pepper, diced
3/4 c. red pepper, diced
1/2 c. onion, diced

1-1/2 c. shredded Cheddar cheese
1-1/2 c. shredded mozzarella cheese
8 eggs
2/3 c. milk
salt and pepper to taste

Spray a 13"x9" baking pan with non-stick vegetable spray. Lightly press crescent rolls into pan, pinching seams together and gently pulling to cover bottom of pan; set aside. Brown sausage in a skillet over medium heat. Drain and sprinkle over crescent rolls; set aside. Melt butter in a separate skillet over medium heat. Add peppers and onion; cook for about 10 to 12 minutes. Spoon pepper mixture evenly over sausage; top with cheeses. In a large bowl, beat eggs with milk, salt and pepper. Evenly spoon egg mixture over all. Bake, uncovered, at 350 degrees for 30 to 35 minutes. Allow to cool slightly; cut into squares. Makes 8 to 10 servings.

A fun countdown to Christmas! Get the family together and think up 24 fun holiday activities like making gingerbread cookies for classmates, dancing to holiday music, sledding or reading a Christmas story. Write each on a calendar for December, then do the activities together.

Morning Pecan Casserole

Barbara Topp
Sparta, NJ

Need a great recipe to serve on Christmas morning or any morning that you have overnight guests staying with you? This recipe is delicious and easy to make ahead the night before.

16-oz. loaf raisin bread, cubed
7-oz. pkg. brown & serve pork
   sausage links
6 eggs
1-1/2 c. milk
1-1/2 c. half-and-half
1 t. vanilla extract

1/4 t. nutmeg
1/2 t. cinnamon
1 c. brown sugar, packed
1/2 c. butter, melted
2 T. maple syrup
1 c. chopped pecans

Spray a 13"x9" baking pan with non-stick vegetable spray. Add bread cubes to pan; set aside. Brown sausage in a skillet over medium heat; drain and cut into bite-size pieces. Add sausage to bread cubes; mix well. In a large bowl, beat eggs, milk, half-and-half, vanilla and spices until blended. Pour over bread mixture. Cover with plastic wrap; refrigerate overnight. Just before baking, combine remaining ingredients in a bowl; mix well and spoon evenly over casserole. Bake, uncovered, at 350 degrees for 40 minutes, or until bubbly and golden. Makes 8 servings.

As a child in the 40s and 50s, I sometimes got into things and was told, "You'd better be good or you will get a lump of coal in your stocking!" With a coal bin in our basement, I thought maybe that could be true. I tried to be good those weeks before Christmas but still I would get into things. Nervous about the upcoming Christmas morning...did I dare go into the living room? I stretched and yawned and bravely went to the Christmas tree to see what Santa had left. Whew! One more year gone by and fruit, candy and toys in my stocking. What a relief! I promised myself I would try to be good in the coming year.

–Sandy Coffey, Cincinnati, OH

Apricot-Almond Coffee Cake

Wendy Ball
Battle Creek, MI

Way back when we were first married, I didn't have a Bundt® pan or a tube pan at the time, but did have a cake pan, so I converted this recipe to make in my cake pan. So, for Christmas I asked for some new pans, and I got them!

2 c. plus 1 T. all-purpose flour, divided
1 c. butter, softened
2 c. sugar
3 eggs
8-oz. container sour cream
1 t. almond extract
1 t. baking powder
1/4 t. salt
12-oz. jar apricot preserves, divided
3/4 c. sliced almonds, divided

Spray a 13"x9" baking pan with non-stick vegetable spray. Sprinkle with one tablespoon flour; set aside. In a large bowl, blend butter and sugar. Add eggs, one at a time, sour cream and extract; mix well. In a separate bowl, mix remaining flour, baking powder and salt; add to blended mixture and stir well. Spread half of batter in pan. Spread half of preserves to within 1/2 inch of edges. Sprinkle with half of almonds. Repeat layers. Bake at 350 degrees for 55 to 60 minutes, until a toothpick inserted near center comes out clean. While cake is cooling, make Glaze. Drizzle Glaze over coffee cake and allow to cool. Serve slightly warm. Makes 12 servings.

Glaze:

2 c. powdered sugar
1/2 t. almond extract
2 to 3 T. milk

Combine powdered sugar, extract and 2 tablespoons milk. Add additional milk, as needed, for a drizzling consistency.

A merry Christmas to us all, my dears!

–Charles Dickens

Fa-La-La Frittata

Amy Hunt
Traphill, NC

This is a terrific Christmas Eve brunch meal to share with family & friends. If you don't have an ovenproof skillet, wrap the handle in a double layer of aluminum foil.

2 T. olive oil
1/2 c. onion, diced
5 eggs
1/4 c. milk
6-oz. jar marinated artichokes,
   drained and diced

1/2 c. pitted Kalamata olives,
   diced
1/4 c. red pepper, finely diced
1/4 t. pepper
2 c. shredded sharp Cheddar
   cheese, divided

Heat oil in a non-stick ovenproof skillet over medium heat. Add onion; cook until tender. In a bowl, beat eggs and milk until blended. Stir in remaining ingredients except cheese; mix well. Stir in one cup cheese. Pour mixture over onion mixture in skillet; mix well. Cook over medium heat for 2 minutes. Transfer skillet to oven. Bake, uncovered, at 350 degrees for 14 minutes, or until center is just set. Sprinkle with remaining cheese. Bake for 2 more minutes, or cheese is melted. Cut into wedges to serve. Serves 6.

Roasted New Potatoes

Melanie Taynor
Everett, WA

Better than hashbrowns! Garnish with sprigs of fresh rosemary.

1/4 c. butter, melted
garlic powder, seasoned salt and
   pepper to taste

2 t. fresh rosemary
1-1/2 lbs. new potatoes,
   cut into wedges

In a shallow 13"x9" baking pan, combine butter and seasonings. Add potatoes; stir to coat evenly. Arrange the potatoes in a single layer. Bake, uncovered, at 350 degrees until potatoes are golden, about 20 to 25 minutes, stirring occasionally. Makes 4 servings.

Overnight Egg Fondue

Violet Leonard
Chesapeake, VA

My mom used to make this every Christmas morning and now I do too. I'm not sure when the name came from, but it's a delicious breakfast casserole. It's so easy to make the night before, refrigerate, then pop in the oven before everyone gets up to open gifts.

12 slices bread
1/4 c. butter, softened
6 slices American cheese
2 c. bacon, ham or sausage,
    cooked and chopped

6 eggs
3 c. milk
1/2 t. salt
1/2 t. pepper

Spread bread slices on one side with butter. Place 6 slices butter-side down in a lightly greased 13"x9" baking pan. Top each with a cheese slice; top with meat. Add remaining bread slices, butter-side up. In a bowl, beat eggs with milk, salt and pepper; pour over all. Cover with aluminum foil; refrigerate overnight. In the morning, bake, covered, at 350 degrees for 50 to 60 minutes. Uncover during last 10 to 15 minutes to brown the top. Serves 6 to 8.

Bacon-Wrapped Pineapple Bites

Kendall Hale
Lynn, MA

Sweet and savory morsels for your Christmas buffet.

1 lb. thin-sliced bacon, halved
20-oz. can pineapple chunks,
    drained

3 T. dark brown sugar, packed

Wrap one half-slice bacon around each pineapple chunk. Place on a wire rack in an aluminum foil-lined baking sheet. Bake at 375 degrees for 20 minutes. Sprinkle with brown sugar. Broil for several minutes, watching closely. Cool slightly. Serves 6 to 8.

Cinnamon Cheese Straws

Virginia Craven
Denton, TX

I like to make and freeze these tasty treats the day before. Later, all I have to do is dip in butter and cinnamon-sugar and bake. If I have a really busy morning, these can be baked a day ahead and served at room temperature. They are delicious both ways.

16-oz. loaf thin-sliced white
    bread, crusts trimmed
8-oz. pkg. regular or low-fat
    cream cheese, softened

1 c. butter, melted
1 T. cinnamon
2 c. sugar

Roll each slice of bread flat with a rolling pin. If bread sticks to rolling pin, cover bread with wax paper or parchment paper before rolling. Spread a thin amount of cream cheese on each slice; cut in half diagonally. Roll up each half-slice from long end to small end, crescent-style. Place in a freezer container; cover and freeze. To serve, place melted butter in a dish; combine cinnamon and sugar in a separate dish. Dip each frozen crescent in melted butter; roll in cinnamon-sugar. Arrange on parchment paper-lined baking sheets. Bake at 350 degrees for 20 to 25 minutes, until lightly golden. Serve warm or at room temperature. Makes about 2 dozen.

Invite the new neighbors or the new family at church over for a holiday brunch. Send them home with a basket of fresh-baked goodies wrapped in a tea towel...what a friendly gesture!

Gingerbread Pancakes

Courtney Stultz
Weir, KS

Pancakes are a huge hit at our house...especially in our favorite holiday shapes! We always serve brunch on Christmas morning at our house and these make such festive treats.

3/4 c. milk
1/2 c. strong brewed coffee,
   slightly cooled
1 egg, beaten
1-1/2 c. all-purpose flour
1 t. baking powder

1/4 t. salt
2 t. ground ginger
1 t. cinnamon
1/2 t. allspice
Garnish: maple syrup or
   powdered sugar

In a large bowl, combine all ingredients except garnish. Beat with an electric mixer on medium speed for about 30 seconds, until well combined. If batter is too runny, add a little more flour; if it is too dry, add a little more milk. Place greased metal cookie cutters onto a hot griddle over medium heat; slowly pour batter into cutters. Cook on first side about 10 minutes. Turn over pancakes and cutters; cook on other side for about 5 minutes. Carefully remove pancakes from cookie cutters. Serve with maple syrup or powdered sugar. Makes 8 to 10 servings.

Mix up some figgy butter to serve with waffles, pancakes and scones. In a bowl, combine one cup softened butter with one cup fig preserves, 1/2 teaspoon vanilla extract and 1/8 teaspoon nutmeg. Mix well. Transfer to a sheet of parchment paper, roll into a log and chill for at least one hour. To serve, simply slice off what you need.

Mom's Blueberry Panakuchen

Holly Epperson
Olive Branch, MS

This was my mother's recipe...she made it every Sunday morning, with fresh berries of any kind. The wonderful smell in the kitchen always enticed everyone to wake up!

4 eggs, beaten
1 c. milk
1 t. orange zest
1/2 t. vanilla extract
1/4 c. sugar

1 c. all-purpose flour
2 T. butter, sliced
1 c. fresh blueberries
Garnish: powdered sugar

Place a cast-iron skillet in a 400-degree oven to warm. Meanwhile, in a large bowl, whisk together eggs and milk. Add orange zest and vanilla; mix well. Add sugar and flour; whisk until completely combined. Allow batter to rest for a few minutes. Carefully remove hot skillet from oven and add butter, swirling in the pan until completely melted. Pour batter into pan; sprinkle blueberries all over the top. Bake at 400 degrees for 20 minutes, or until pancake is puffed and cooked through. Dust with powdered sugar; cut into wedges and serve immediately. Makes 4 servings.

Yes, Virginia, there is a Santa Claus. He exists as certainly as love and generosity and devotion exist, and you know that they abound and give to your life its highest beauty and joy.

–Francis P. Church

Christmas Breakfast Casserole

Maggie Clark
Kansas City, MO

For as long as I can remember, this dish has been my go-to recipe for Christmas morning brunch. Served with a mixed fruit salad, coffee cake and mimosas, it gives the whole family a hearty start before the frantic unwrapping of packages begins.

8-oz. tube refrigerated crescent
    rolls
8-oz. pkg. brown & serve pork
    sausage links, sliced
2 c. shredded Swiss cheese
4 eggs, lightly beaten

3/4 c. milk
1 T. green pepper, diced
1 T. red pepper, diced
1/2 t. dried oregano
1/2 t. salt
1/2 t. pepper

Separate crescent rolls into 2 large rectangles; place in an ungreased 13"x9" baking pan. Press over the bottom and 1/2-inch up the sides to form a crust. Arrange sliced sausages over crust; top with cheese. Combine remaining ingredients in a bowl; whisk well and pour over cheese. Bake, uncovered, at 425 degrees for 20 to 25 minutes, until golden. Makes 5 to 6 servings.

Stir up a batch of mimosas for a special brunch. For each serving, combine 3/4 cup chilled champagne and 1/4 cup orange juice. Little ones can enjoy their own version made with ginger ale and orange juice.

Ho-Ho-Ho Breakfast Pizza

Elizabeth Smithson
Cunningham, KY

I got this recipe from our extension agent years ago and it's still our favorite for Christmas morning. The kids loved it still and now the grandkids love it. So easy.

1 lb. ground pork sausage
8-oz. tube refrigerated crescent
   rolls
1 c. shredded Cheddar cheese
1 c. shredded mozzarella cheese
6 eggs, beaten

1/2 c. milk
3/4 t. dried oregano
1/8 t. pepper
Garnish: sliced red and green
   peppers

Cook sausage in a skillet over medium heat until browned; drain and set aside. Meanwhile, separate crescent rolls into 8 triangles. Arrange triangles in a greased 12" round pizza pan, with elongated points toward center. Press bottom and sides to form a crust; seal perforations. Bake crust at 350 degrees for 5 minutes, until puffy. Sprinkle sausage over dough; top with cheeses. In a bowl, whisk together eggs, milk and seasonings; pour over all. Bake at 350 degrees for 30 to 35 minutes. Cut into wedges; garnish with red and green pepper slices. Makes 6 to 8 servings.

It is rare that we have a white Christmas in the south. But one year when I was little, we did! We didn't have a fireplace for Santa to enter, so my dad would leave a window open just a little. Christmas morning I would find a piece of torn, red velvet material stuck to a nail on the window sill. Poor Santa had ripped his coat! Dad also made the carrots that we left the reindeer look partially eaten. Outdoors, he even made tracks in the snow showing where the reindeer and sleigh runners had been. He made a true believer out of me!

–Dottie Dziurkowski, Royal, AR

Christmas Comfort Classics

Jolly Breakfast Ring

Vickie

*This recipe is such fun...it looks like a Christmas wreath!
I found this gem years ago in a hometown cookbook.*

4 T. butter, melted and divided
2 T. brown sugar, packed
12 maraschino cherries, chopped
7 T. chopped walnuts, divided

1/2 c. sugar
1 t. cinnamon
2 c. biscuit baking mix
2/3 c. milk

Brush 2 tablespoons butter in an angel food cake pan. Sprinkle brown sugar, cherries and 4 tablespoons walnuts into bottom of pan; set aside. In a small bowl, mix remaining walnuts, sugar and cinnamon; set aside. In a large bowl, combine biscuit mix and milk. Stir with a fork; beat for 15 strokes, until stiff. Form dough into 12 balls. Roll each ball in remaining butter, then in walnut mixture. Arrange balls in pan. Bake at 400 degrees for 25 to 30 minutes, until golden. Turn out onto a plate; serve warm. Makes 12 servings.

Ruby Red Frost

*Carolyn Deckard
Bedford, IN*

We always serve this at Christmas. It was Mom's favorite.

2 c. cranberry juice cocktail
1-1/2 c. lemon juice
1 c. sugar
1 pt. raspberry sherbet

2 28-oz. bottles ginger ale,
  chilled
Optional: lemon slices

In a pitcher, combine fruit juices and sugar; stir well. Chill. Add sherbet and ginger ale just before serving. Garnish with lemon slices, if desired.

Christmas! The very word brings joy to our hearts.

–Joan Winmill Brown

16

Norwegian Kringla

Delci Whalen
Coeur D'Alene, ID

This delectable pastry with its almond glaze is a tradition for our family every Christmas morning! There is never any left.

2 c. all-purpose flour, divided
1 c. margarine, divided
1 c. plus 1 T. water, divided

3 eggs
1-1/2 t. almond extract

In a bowl, combine one cup flour, 1/2 cup margarine and one tablespoon water. Mix with a fork; work well with hands. Roll dough into 2 ropes. Pat out on a greased baking sheet into 2 long strips, each 3 inches wide; set aside. To a heavy saucepan, add remaining water and remaining margarine; bring to a boil. Remove from heat. Add remaining flour; stir in eggs, one at a time, and extract. Mix until smooth; spread evenly over dough strips. Bake at 375 degrees for 45 minutes. Remove from oven; let cool. Drizzle Frosting over pastries. Cut into one-inch strips. Serves 8.

Frosting:

1 c. powdered sugar
1 T. milk

1 T. butter, melted
1/2 t. almond extract

Combine all ingredients; stir to a drizzling consistency.

Remember the birds at Christmastime. Decorate an outdoor tree with birdseed bells, suet balls, garlands of fruit and hollowed-out orange halves filled with birdseed.

Apple-Filled Oven French Toast

Sue Klapper
Muskego, WI

I always serve this to my family on Christmas morning. It is so delicious...almost a dessert! If I am feeling really decadent I top each piece with a dollop of whipped cream. I love that I can make it the night before I serve it, and I don't even have to peel and chop the apples. You will love it too!

1 to 2 T. butter, softened	2 c. milk
12-oz. loaf French bread, sliced 1-inch thick and divided	2 c. half-and-half
21-oz. can apple pie filling	2 t. vanilla extract
8 eggs	1/2 t. nutmeg
	1/2 t. cinnamon

Spread butter generously in a 13"x9" baking pan. Arrange half of bread slices in pan in a single layer; spread pie filling over bread. Arrange remaining bread on top; set aside. In a blender, combine remaining ingredients. Process until smooth; pour over bread. Cover and refrigerate overnight. Just before baking, uncover and spread Topping over top. Bake at 350 degrees for 50 minutes, or until golden. Serves 6 to 8.

Topping:

1/2 c. butter, softened	2 T. corn syrup
1 c. brown sugar, packed	1 c. chopped nuts

Combine all ingredients; mix well.

Clip vintage Christmas cards onto pine garland with
red clothespins for a festive mantel decoration.

Cinnamon-Walnut Coffee Cake *Mel Chencharick*
Julian, PA

Even though this is a made-from-scratch coffee cake, it only takes about 15 to 20 minutes of prep time. Perfect for any morning when you have a few extra minutes!

2 c. all-purpose flour
3/4 t. baking soda
1/2 t. salt
1 c. buttermilk
1/4 c. oil
1 egg, beaten

1 t. vanilla extract
1-1/2 c. sugar, divided
1-1/2 c. chopped walnuts
1 T. cinnamon
1/3 c. powdered sugar
2 to 2-1/2 t. milk

In a bowl, combine flour, baking soda and salt; set aside. In a large bowl, combine buttermilk, oil, egg, vanilla and 3/4 cup sugar. Add flour mixture; beat until just moistened. Spread half of batter into a greased 8"x8" baking pan; set aside. In a small bowl, combine walnuts, remaining sugar and cinnamon. Sprinkle 1-1/2 cups of walnut mixture over batter. Spread with remaining batter; top with remaining walnut mixture. Cut through batter with a knife to swirl. Bake at 350 degrees for 35 to 40 minutes, until a toothpick inserted near the center comes out clean. Stir together powdered sugar and milk; drizzle over coffee cake. Serve warm, or cool on a wire rack. Cut into squares. Serves 9.

Sparkly sticks of rock candy are fun for stirring
hot beverages.

Christmas Comfort Classics

Christmas Brunch Coffee Punch
Jodi Spires
Centerville, OH

Christmas wouldn't be Christmas without this punch at our family celebrations! If you like iced coffee, cappuccino and similar drinks, you will love it! I host a ladies' Christmas brunch every year and it's always a big hit with the ladies too.

2 c. water
2 c. sugar
1/4 c. instant coffee granules
1/2 gal. milk

1/2 gal. chocolate ice cream, slightly softened
1/2 gal. vanilla ice cream, slightly softened

In a saucepan, bring water to a boil over high heat. Add sugar; stir to dissolve. Turn off heat. Add coffee; stir to dissolve completely. Cool; pour into a covered container and refrigerate for several hours to overnight. At serving time, pour cold coffee mixture into a large punch bowl. Add milk and ice creams; stir to combine. Stir punch occasionally as ice cream continues to melt. Serves 12 to 15.

Mother's Almond Tea
Debbie Driggers
Campbell, TX

My mother always made this tea at the holidays. It is delicious...always a special family favorite!

6 c. water
2 c. sugar
1/4 c. lemon juice
46-oz. can pineapple juice
3 c. strong brewed tea

1/2 c. powdered orange drink mix
1-1/2 t. almond extract
1-1/2 t. vanilla extract

In a saucepan over high heat, combine water, sugar and lemon juice. Simmer for 5 minutes, stirring often; cool. Stir in remaining ingredients. Serve hot or cold. Freezes well also. Makes about one gallon.

Family Tradition Cinnamon Rolls

Vicky Blackmore
Holliston, MA

For every Christmas morning I can remember, I have had these cinnamon rolls for breakfast. Mom always made them for my sisters and brother and me. Now I make a double batch for my family... extra icing is always appreciated too!

2 c. all-purpose flour
1 T. baking powder
1 t. salt
8 T. butter, softened and divided

2/3 c. milk
1/4 c. sugar
1 t. cinnamon

In a bowl, mix together flour, baking powder and salt. With a knife, cut in 6 tablespoons butter finely; stir in milk to make a soft dough. Knead dough lightly for about 30 seconds on a lightly floured surface. Roll out dough into a 16-inch by 7-inch rectangle, 1/4-inch thick. Spread with remaining butter. Sprinkle with sugar and cinnamon. Roll up tightly, beginning on one wide edge. Seal well by pinching edge of dough into roll. Cut into one-inch slices; place slices cut-side down on greased baking sheets. May be covered and frozen at this point, if desired. Bake at 425 degrees for about 15 minutes, checking often toward the end to avoid burning. Drizzle Icing over warm rolls when they come out of the oven. Makes 16 rolls.

Icing:

1/2 c. powdered sugar
1/4 t. vanilla extract

1-1/2 t. milk

Combine all ingredients, adding milk slowly to get a drizzling consistency.

Tie tiny Christmas ornaments onto stemmed glasses with ribbon bows...so festive at a holiday brunch.

Pineapple Scones

Margaret Welder
Madrid, IA

My mother taught me the love of cooking, and as a result I have taught cooking classes at businesses and our church for many years. I love to try out new ideas and recipes. This one is a favorite of mine...I have had numerous requests for this recipe.

2-1/2 c. all-purpose flour
1/2 c. sugar
2 t. baking powder
1/2 t. salt
1/2 c. butter, softened
3-oz. pkg. cream cheese,
　softened

1 c. dried pineapple, finely
　diced
2 T. toasted pecans, chopped
1/3 c. whipping cream
Optional: raw or granulated
　sugar

In a large bowl, combine flour, sugar, baking powder and salt; mix well. Cut in butter and cream cheese with a fork or 2 knives until crumbly. Stir in pineapple, nuts and cream. Turn out dough onto a floured board. Pat or roll out to 3/4-inch thick. With a biscuit cutter, cut into 2-inch rounds. Sprinkle with sugar, if desired. Place on a parchment paper-lined baking sheet. Bake at 375 degrees for 15 minutes, or until golden. Makes 8 scones.

Make Mock Devonshire Cream to spoon onto warm scones... it's irresistible! Blend a 3-ounce package of cream cheese with one tablespoon sugar and 1/8 teaspoon salt. Stir in one cup whipping cream. Beat with an electric mixer on high speed until fluffy and stiff peaks form. Keep refrigerated.

White Chocolate-Cherry Scones
Cheri Maxwell
Gulf Breeze, FL

My best girlfriends and I always get together for a simple brunch in December, then go Christmas shopping. We especially like these yummy scones!

3 c. all-purpose flour
1/2 c. sugar
2-1/2 t. baking powder
1/2 t. baking soda
6 T. butter, softened

1 c. vanilla yogurt
6 T. milk, divided
1-1/3 c. sweetened dried
　cherries
2/3 c. white chocolate chips

In a large bowl, combine flour, sugar, baking powder and baking soda. Cut in butter with a fork until mixture resembles coarse crumbs; set aside. In a small bowl, combine yogurt and 4 tablespoons milk. Stir into crumb mixture just until moistened. Mix in cherries and chocolate chips. Pat dough into a 9-inch circle on an ungreased baking sheet. Cut into 8 wedges; gently separate wedges. Brush with remaining milk. Bake at 400 degrees for 20 to 25 minutes, until golden. Makes 8 scones.

Turn refrigerated cinnamon rolls into snowmen. Arrange rolls in a snowman shape on a baking sheet and bake as directed. Top with fluffy white icing and add faces with bits of dried fruit or mini candies. Festive and fun!

Slow-Cooker Apple Oats

LaDeana Cooper
Batavia, OH

Last winter, when I heard of a good snowstorm moving in, I knew the kids would be "up and at 'em!" So, I wanted them to have something hot and hearty to warm their tummies before heading out. They absolutely loved it and ask me to make it year 'round. The steel-cut oats give the dish a nutty taste. I hope you and your family enjoy it as much as mine does!

2 apples, peeled if desired,
   cored and chopped
2 c. milk
1-1/2 c. water
1/4 c. brown sugar, packed

1/2 c. unsweetened applesauce
1 c. steel-cut oats, uncooked
1 T. butter
1 t. cinnamon
1/4 t. salt

Spray a 6-quart slow cooker with non-stick vegetable spray, if desired. Combine all ingredients in slow cooker; stir to combine. Cover and cook on low setting for 7 hours. Stir again before serving. Makes 6 servings.

Help the kids mix up some "Magic Reindeer Food" just for fun! Fill a plastic sandwich bag with a big spoonful of uncooked oats, a dash of sugar and some candy sprinkles. On Christmas Eve they can sprinkle it on the lawn to guide Santa's reindeer to your home.

Pearl's Christmas Morning Parfait

Barbara Bradham
Carlsbad, CA

Over 50 years ago, my mother tried this refreshing recipe on Christmas morning, and our family has been sharing it ever since. Each generation has adopted it and continues the celebration. My daughters have lived all over the world and each Christmas morning, no matter what country they were in, Pearl's Christmas Morning Parfait was served. I hope your family enjoys this fun, easy treat too.

1/2 c. corn flake cereal
1/2 c. frozen strawberries,
   thawed

1/2 c. vanilla ice cream,
   thawed

In a tall clear parfait glass or large stemmed glass, layer cereal, ice cream and strawberries until glass is full. Serve immediately. Makes one serving; make as many as you want.

My favorite Christmas memory is of sleeping in sleeping bags under the lit Christmas tree every December 23rd when my kids were little. They would get so excited about laying their sleeping bags just so, then all the lights would be turned off until we had just the glow of the tree to illuminate their chubby little faces. They are teens now and no longer interested in sleeping under the tree anymore, so I fondly look at photos of when they were small and everything Christmas excited them, while I sit in the glow of the tree.

–Sara Crocker, Rochester, WA

Gen's Shrimp Creole

Gen Cornish
Arizona City, AZ

This is such a delicious, quick-to-make recipe. For an elegant holiday breakfast or brunch, I serve it spooned over egg omelets. I like to make a couple batches and freeze them in pint containers.

1/2 c. green pepper, chopped
1/2 c. onion, chopped
2 T. butter
14-1/2 oz. can stewed tomatoes
1/2 t. sugar
1/2 t. chili powder
1/8 t. garlic powder

1/8 t. dried thyme
1/16 t. cayenne pepper
1/2 bay leaf
salt and pepper to taste
20 to 30 frozen uncooked
    shrimp, cleaned and thawed
cooked rice

In a skillet over medium heat, sauté pepper and onion in butter until crisp-tender. Add tomatoes with juice and seasonings. Reduce heat to medium-low; simmer for 20 minutes. Add shrimp and cook until no longer transparent, about 3 to 4 minutes. Discard bay leaf. Serve over cooked rice. Makes 4 servings.

Planning a midday brunch? Alongside breakfast foods like baked eggs, coffee cake and muffins, offer a light, savory main dish or two for those who have already enjoyed breakfast.

Country Club Eggs

Marian Forck
Chamois, MO

*This is a very special overnight casserole that everyone loves.
It is so good warmed up the next day, if you are lucky to
have some left over! Try it with crisp bacon too...delicious!*

5 slices bread, cubed
1/2 to 1 lb. ground pork sausage
8-oz. pkg. shredded mild
    Cheddar cheese, divided
1/2 c. mushrooms, chopped
1/2 c. onion, chopped

1 T. butter
5 eggs, beaten
2 c. milk
1/4 t. dry mustard
1/4 t. dried sage
1/8 t. salt

Spread bread cubes over the bottom of a greased 13"x9" baking pan;
set aside. Brown sausage in a skillet over medium heat; drain well.
Sprinkle sausage over bread cubes; sprinkle half of cheese over
sausage and set aside. Wipe out skillet; sauté mushrooms and onion
in butter. Meanwhile, whisk together eggs, milk and seasonings in a
bowl; pour over sausage. Sprinkle with mushroom mixture and
remaining cheese. Cover with aluminum foil; refrigerate overnight.
Loosen foil; bake at 350 degrees for one hour. Take foil off for last
15 minutes. Serves 6 to 8.

Vintage salt & pepper shakers, in the shape of snowmen or
Mr. & Mrs. Santa, add a touch of holiday cheer to any
buffet table and a smile to guests' faces.

Turkey Fruit Salad

Patricia Wissler
Harrisburg, PA

We have served this recipe many times for women's brunches
at church. It's always a hit!

1/2 c. mayonnaise
2 T. honey
1/8 t. ground ginger
2 c. cooked turkey, diced
11-oz. can mandarin oranges,
    drained

8-1/4 oz. can pineapple chunks,
    drained
1 c. apple, cored and chopped
1 c. seedless grapes, halved
1/2 c. pecan halves, toasted

In a large bowl, combine mayonnaise, honey and ginger. Stir in remaining ingredients except pecans. Cover and refrigerate for one hour. Sprinkle with pecans just before serving. Makes 8 servings.

Little Pecan Muffins

Kathy Grashoff
Fort Wayne, IN

If you are having a brunch or a party this holiday season,
these sweet little muffins will speed you on your way...
just look how many this recipe makes!

1 c. light brown sugar, packed
1/2 c. butter, melted
2 eggs, beaten

1 t. vanilla extract
1 c. chopped pecans
1/2 c. all-purpose flour

Combine brown sugar, melted butter, eggs and vanilla; beat until smooth. Stir in pecans and flour. Spoon batter into mini muffin cups sprayed with non-stick vegetable spray, filling 3/4 full. Bake at 375 degrees for 12 minutes, or until lightly golden. Cool in pans on wire racks for one minute. Remove muffins from pans; cool completely on a wire rack. Makes about 3 dozen.

A baker's secret! Grease muffin cups on the bottoms and just halfway up the sides. Muffins will bake up nicely puffed on top.

Hot Fruit Bake

Donna Wilson
Maryville, TN

This is our family's Christmas breakfast tradition. It smells wonderful baking as we open gifts.

21-oz. can cherry pie filling
20-oz. jar chunky applesauce
18-oz. can pineapple chunks, drained
15-oz. sliced peaches, drained

15-oz. can mandarin oranges, drained
1/2 c. brown sugar, packed
1 t. cinnamon
1/2 t. allspice

In a bowl, mix all ingredients together. Pour into an ungreased 2-quart casserole dish. Bake, uncovered, at 350 degrees for one hour, or until hot and bubbly. Makes 8 servings.

Raspberry Cheese Danish

Nancy Wise
Little Rock, AR

A yummy little treat you can whip up in a few minutes.

8-oz. tube refrigerated crescent rolls
1/4 c. cream cheese, softened

3/4 c. powdered sugar, divided
4 T. raspberry jam, divided
2 t. milk

Separate crescent rolls into 4 rectangles; press together seams. Cut in half to make 8 squares. In a bowl, blend cream cheese with 1/4 cup powdered sugar. Spread one tablespoon cheese mixture down the center of each square; top with one tablespoon jam. Bring 2 opposite corners together; press to seal. Place on a parchment paper-lined baking sheet. Bake at 375 degrees for 10 to 12 minutes, until golden. Combine remaining powdered sugar with milk; drizzle over top. Makes 4 servings.

Go ahead and unpack the Christmas tableware early in December...even the simplest meal is special when served on holly-trimmed plates.

Iced Spiced Ginger Bars

Darlene Hartzler
Marshallville, OH

*These bars are so flavorful and moist...wonderful with
a cup of hot coffee on a cold winter morning.*

2 c. all-purpose flour
1 c. sugar
1 t. baking soda
1 t. cinnamon
1 t. ground ginger
1 t. ground cloves

1/8 t. salt
1 c. hot brewed coffee
1/2 c. butter, softened
1/2 c. shortening
1/2 c. molasses
2 eggs, beaten

Combine all ingredients in a bowl. Beat with an electric mixer
on medium speed until well mixed. Pour batter into a greased
13"x9" baking pan. Bake at 350 degrees for 25 to 30 minutes,
until top springs back when touched lightly in center. Cool. Spread
with Frosting; cut into bars. Makes 3 dozen.

Frosting:

1/3 c. butter, sliced
3 c. powdered sugar

1/2 t. vanilla extract
3 to 4 T. water

In a small saucepan over low heat, stirring constantly, cook butter
until lightly golden. Stir in remaining ingredients until smooth.

Small drawstring bags sewn of holiday print fabric are
sweet table favors. Fill them with packets of flavored
tea or coffee for a special surprise.

Tree Trimming
Open House

Warm Cranberry-Honey Brie

Delores Lakes
Mansfield, OH

I always just have to make this simple appetizer for
our family. It's one of our son's favorites and a prelude
to our Christmas dinner!

5-oz. pkg. round Brie cheese
2 T. sweetened dried cranberries
1 t. fresh thyme, chopped

1 t. chopped walnuts, toasted
1 T. honey
favorite crackers

With a serrated knife, remove top rind from cheese. Place cheese,
cut-side up, in a one-quart casserole dish. Evenly sprinkle cheese with
cranberries, thyme and walnuts. Drizzle with honey. Bake, uncovered,
at 350 degrees for about 20 minutes, until cheese is softened to desired
consistency. Serve warm with crackers. Serves 8.

Invite everyone to a tree-trimming party! Play your favorite
holiday music, serve lots of yummy snacks, and before
you know it everyone will be in the holiday spirit.

Roasted Red Pepper Spread

Donna Cannon
Tulsa, OK

For years, my large Italian family would come together at one of our homes for Christmas Eve or post-Christmas get-togethers. I have eleven brothers and sisters, and there are 44 grandchildren and 46 great-grandchildren! We each signed up to bring appetizers, main dishes, side dishes, desserts and beverages. This roasted red pepper spread was always a favorite.

8-oz. container mayonnaise
8-oz. container sour cream
7-oz. jar roasted red peppers,
    drained and liquid reserved
1 handful fresh basil, loosely
    packed

salt and pepper to taste
Melba toast rounds, snack
    crackers, vegetable slices

In a food processor, combine mayonnaise and sour cream. Add peppers, basil, salt and pepper; pulse until well-combined. Blend in reserved liquid, one tablespoon at a time, to desired consistency. Spoon into a serving dish or bread bowl. Serve with Melba toast, crackers or vegetables. Makes 2 to 3 cups.

Scooped-out red and green peppers make fun containers
for dips and sauces.

Holiday Cheese Ball

*Patty Burkemper
Rossemount, MN*

My mother used to make this cheese ball recipe every year at Christmastime. With finely chopped red and green peppers, it looks especially festive. Everyone who tastes it begs for the recipe, so I am happy to share it with you.

2 8-oz. pkgs. cream cheese, softened
8-oz. pkg, sharp Cheddar cheese, shredded
1 T. green pepper, minced
1 T. red pepper, minced

1 t. onion, minced
1 t. lemon juice
2 t. Worcestershire sauce
1/8 t. cayenne pepper
1/8 t. salt
Garnish: finely chopped pecans

In a large bowl, blend cream cheese with shredded cheese. Add remaining ingredients except garnish; blend all together. Shape into a ball; wrap in wax paper. Chill for 24 hours. Just before serving, roll in pecans. Makes 8 to 10 servings.

I don't think anyone loved Christmas as much as my father.
I remember one year, especially, he was even more excited
for us kids to open our gifts than we were. He pulled us out of
bed immediately after "Santa came" and had us all up, opening gifts
at 2AM on Christmas morning. He's been gone for 30 years now, but
that joy never left me and I often find myself up before the kids on
Christmas morning, just waiting and thinking of Dad.

–Colleen Ludgate, Ontario, Canada

Pub Cheese Spread

Raelene Wilson
Claremont, NH

I have had this recipe since the early 70s. I was at a wedding where a crock of this spread was served on each guest table. We all raved about it and were sent a copy along with our thank-you notes.

12-oz. container Cheddar cheese spread
8-oz. pkg. cream cheese
1-1/2 t. garlic powder, or more to taste
12-oz. can regular or non-alcoholic beer
buttery round crackers or shredded wheat crackers

Combine cheeses in a large bowl to soften. With an electric mixer on low speed, beat in garlic powder. Beat in beer, one tablespoon at a time, to desired consistency. Transfer to a serving bowl; cover and chill. Serve with crackers. Makes 10 to 12 servings.

Spoon your secret-recipe dip or spread into a vintage canning jar...an ideal hostess gift. Add a box of crisp crackers and tie on a spreader with a pretty ribbon. Sure to be appreciated!

Cheese & Tomato Puffs

Jennifer Niemi
Nova Scotia, Canada

These puffs are very festive looking and delicious but really, really easy to make. Great for a New Year's Day brunch, lunch or even dinner. Serve with a tossed salad, rolls and a glass of wine.

8-oz. pkg. cream cheese,
  softened
1/3 c. grated Parmesan cheese
1 T. tomato paste
2 t. dried basil
1 t. dried oregano
2 t. onion powder

1/8 t. garlic powder
1/8 t. pepper
1/2 t. sugar
2 eggs, divided
1 sheet frozen puff pastry,
  thawed
1 t. milk

In a bowl, blend together cheeses, tomato paste, seasonings and sugar; set aside. Lightly beat one egg; blend into cheese mixture. Set aside. On a lightly floured board, roll out pastry to a 12-inch square. With a knife, cut into 4 pieces, each 6 inches square. Lightly beat remaining egg with milk; brush onto edges of each pastry square in 1-inch thick strips. (Brushed edges will frame 4-inch squares.) Spoon 1/4 of cheese mixture into the center of each pastry square; flatten slightly. Fold pastry squares in half to form rectangles. Press the 3 flat edges of each rectangle firmly to seal. Fold flattened edges over again, sealing together with more egg & milk mixture. Transfer puffs to a greased baking sheet. Brush remaining egg mixture over all exposed surfaces. Bake at 400 degrees for 30 to 35 minutes, or until golden. Makes 4 servings.

For an easy yet elegant appetizer, try a cheese platter. Choose a soft
cheese, a hard cheese and a semi-soft or crumbly cheese.
Add a basket of crisp crackers, crusty baguettes and some
sliced apples or pears. So simple, yet sure to please guests!

Tree Trimming
Open House

Mom's Great Cheese Ball

Patricia Mollohan
Parkersburg, WV

Even though my children are grown, they still come home and spend Christmas Eve with us and stay overnight. Our traditional snacks for Christmas Eve include the Great Cheese Ball, which is my daughter Nichole's favorite. We all enjoy our snacks while setting presents under the tree. I would not trade that time for anything in the world!

2 8-oz. pkgs. cream cheese, softened
2 2-1/2 oz. pkgs. chipped beef or ham, finely chopped and divided
1-oz. pkg. ranch salad dressing mix

1 t. soy sauce
1 t. garlic powder
2 T. dried parsley, divided
assorted crackers

Place cream cheese in a bowl. Add half of beef or ham, dressing mix, soy sauce, garlic powder and one teaspoon parsley. Mix together until well blended; form into a ball and set aside. In a separate bowl, mix together remaining parsley and beef or ham. Roll cheese ball in parsley mixture to coat evenly. Wrap in plastic wrap and refrigerate at least 4 hours; overnight is even better. Serve with assorted crackers. Makes 10 to 20 servings.

"Champagne" Punch

Tracee Cummins
Georgetown, TX

I've had this recipe so long, I can't even remember where it came from. I've made it so many times, I have it memorized!

12-oz. can frozen lemonade concentrate
4 c. water

46-oz. bottle white grape juice
28-oz. bottle ginger ale, chilled

Mix lemonade, water and grape juice in a pitcher; chill. Add ginger ale just before serving. Makes 16 servings.

I am in holiday humor!
–William Shakespeare

Chicken Salad Mini-wiches for a Crowd

Nancy Kailihiwa
Wheatland, CA

I came up with this recipe after being asked to bring a finger food to a holiday party. These little sandwiches were gone in a flash!

3 13-oz. cans chicken breast,
   drained and flaked
6 stalks celery, chopped
24 to 30 seedless grapes,
   quartered
6-oz. can large black olives,
   drained and sliced

1-1/2 c. mayonnaise
2 t. salt
1-1/2 t. pepper
3/4 t. hot pepper sauce
2 t. mustard
24 soft bakery dinner rolls,
   split

In a large bowl, combine all ingredients except rolls; mix very well. Cover and chill. To serve, place a small scoop of chicken salad on each roll. Place on a serving platter. Makes 24 mini sandwiches.

Slip a packet of spiced tea into a Christmas card to a dear friend...she can enjoy a hot cup of tea while reading your latest news.

Baked Mushroom Tarts

Gina Norton
Wonder Lake, IL

*This is my godmother's delicious recipe that she served as
an appetizer at our family Christmas Day celebration.
These savory tarts melt in your mouth.*

5 green onions, minced
4 T. butter
8-oz. can sliced mushrooms,
   drained and minced

salt to taste
1 c. whipping cream
1/2 c. all-purpose flour

Prepare Tart Dough ahead of time; chill. In a skillet over medium heat,
sauté green onions in butter. Add mushrooms; season with salt. In a
separate small saucepan over low heat, whisk cream and flour,
cooking until mixture thickens and turns light tan. Add cream mixture
to mushroom mixture; stir well and remove from heat. Coat your
fingers lightly with flour; shape Tart Dough into one-inch balls. Place
each ball into an ungreased mini muffin cup, pressing into bottom and
sides to form a tart shell. Pierce bottoms of tart shells with a fork.
Spoon mushroom mixture into tart shells. Bake at 450 degrees for
10 to 12 minutes, until lightly golden. Cool tarts in pan for 5 minutes.
Carefully remove to a serving plate. Makes 2 dozen.

Tart Dough:

1/2. c. butter, softened
3-oz. pkg. cream cheese,
   softened

1 c. all-purpose flour

Combine butter and cream cheese in a bowl. Beat with an electric
mixer on medium speed until smooth. Add flour; mix until a soft
dough forms. Cover; chill at least one hour to overnight.

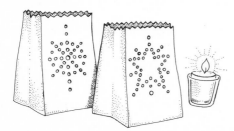

Add a welcoming row of
twinkling luminarias along the
front walk and your house
will be party perfect!

Cheesy Onion Dip

Lynnette Jones
East Flat Rock, NC

A warm, savory slow-cooker dip your guests will love! I like to shake some cracked pepper or paprika on top for added color.

2 c. sweet onions, finely chopped
1-1/4 c. mayonnaise
1-1/2 c. shredded Cheddar cheese
1-1/2 c. grated Parmesan cheese
1/2 c. cream cheese, cut into very small cubes
1-1/2 c. shredded mozzarella cheese
pita chips or snack crackers

In a 3-quart slow cooker, mix onions, mayonnaise, Cheddar cheese and Parmesan cheese. Dot with cream cheese; top with mozzarella cheese. Cover and cook on low setting for 4 to 6 hours. Serve warm with pita chips or crackers. Makes 8 to 10 servings.

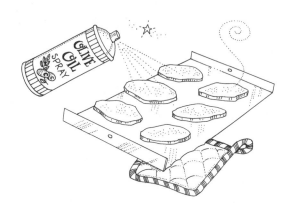

Serve toasty homemade baguette chips with your best cheese spread. Thinly slice a loaf or baguette of French bread. Arrange slices on a baking sheet and spray lightly with non-stick olive oil spray. Bake at 350 degrees for 10 minutes, or until crunchy and golden.

Chili Cheese Dip

Theda Light
Christiansburg, VA

A family in our church invited us to their home and this dip was served. Our hostess gladly gave me the recipe. It is easy to make and oh-so good! This recipe may be doubled and made in a larger slow cooker.

1 lb. lean ground beef
10-oz. can diced tomatoes and
   green chiles
16-oz. pkg. pasteurized process
   cheese spread, cubed

2 t. Worcestershire sauce
1/2 t. chili powder
tortilla chips or scoop-type
   corn chips

Brown beef in a skillet over medium heat; drain. Spoon beef into a 3-quart slow cooker. Add tomatoes with juice, cubed cheese, Worcestershire sauce and chili powder. Cover and cook on high setting for one hour, stirring occasionally, until cheese is fully melted. Serve immediately, or turn to low setting and hold up to 6 hours for serving. Serve with tortilla or corn chips. This recipe may be doubled and made in a larger slow cooker. Serves 8 to 10.

Start a holiday journal...decorate a blank book, then use it to note each year's special moments, guests welcomed, meals enjoyed and gifts given. You'll love looking back on these happy memories!

Veggie Pizza Cups

Jenny Unternahrer
Wayland, IA

These little cups are easy to pick up and eat. I came up with this idea one year after trying to decide what topping to put on the veggie pizza. This way, everyone can have the kind of veggie pizza they like without having to pick off the stuff they don't!

8-oz. tube refrigerated crescent
   rolls
8-oz. pkg. cream cheese,
   softened
1/2 c. sour cream
1/4 t. dried oregano
1/2 t. dried parsley

1/2 t. dill weed
salt and pepper to taste
Garnish: shredded pizza cheese,
   bacon bits, diced carrots,
   green peppers and tomatoes,
   sliced green onions

Roll out crescent rolls; press seams together and cut into 24 equal squares. Turn a mini muffin pan upside-down. Press each square lightly onto the back of a mini muffin cup, using only every other cup to create a checkerboard effect. (Otherwise, dough cups will puff up and stick to each other.) Bake at 375 degrees for 10 to 13 minutes, until golden. Remove cups to a wire rack; set aside. In a bowl, mix together cream cheese, sour cream and seasonings. Spoon mixture into a disposable decorating bag or a plastic zipping bag with a star tip; pipe mixture into cups. Fill a relish tray with toppings as desired, for guests to assemble their own. Makes 2 dozen.

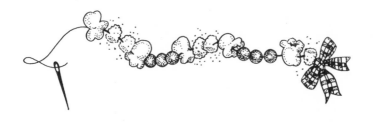

Stringing popcorn is old-fashioned fun! All you need is a
big bowl of plain popcorn, a needle and strong thread.
Add fresh cranberries or even mini gumdrops for color.

Grandma's Christmas Spread

Beth Flack
Terre Haute, IN

Grandma made this spread every Christmas, and my mom and sister both loved it. Now I make it for my sister for Christmas and it has always been a hit at her holiday party.

2 c. finely shredded Cheddar
    cheese
1 c. mayonnaise
1 c. black olives, chopped

2 t. onion, diced
1 loaf party rye bread
3-oz. pkg. bacon bits

In a bowl, combine cheese, mayonnaise, olives and onion; mix well. Spread mixture on bread slices; top with bacon bits. Place slices on a broiler pan. Broil for 4 minutes, or until bubbly and cheese is melted. Makes about 16 servings.

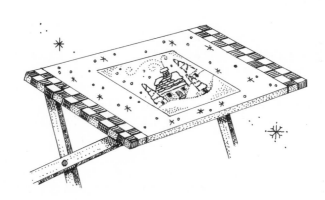

Découpage clippings from Christmas cards onto wooden tray tables...so handy when entertaining!

Tomato-Basil Cheese Ball

Kristin Turner
Raleigh, NC

This recipe is wonderful for entertaining. I wanted a new way to try tomatoes, basil and mozzarella together, so I experimented and this cheese ball turned out to be a hit! I made mine into mini individual cheese balls for my guests and it was perfect!

8-oz. pkg. cream cheese, softened
2 c. shredded Italian-blend cheese
4 t. pesto sauce
4 t. sun-dried tomato pesto sauce
3-oz. pkg. pine nuts, toasted and coarsely chopped
crackers or pita chips

Mix together cheeses and pesto sauces in a large bowl. Shape into a ball; roll in pine nuts. Wrap in plastic wrap; refrigerate until ready to serve. Serve with crackers or pita chips. Makes 12 servings.

Parmesan Herb Pita Chips

Brenda Hager
Nancy, KY

These quick & easy chips can be made ahead. They're good alone or with your favorite holiday dip.

3 6-inch pita rounds
1/3 c. olive oil
4 t. Italian seasoning
1 t. garlic salt
1/2 c. shredded Parmesan cheese

Split each pita into 2 rounds; cut each round into 8 wedges. Combine oil and seasonings; brush mixture over the split side of each wedge. Sprinkle with cheese; arrange on an ungreased baking sheet. Bake at 350 degrees for 10 to 15 minutes, until crisp. Transfer to wire racks to cool. Makes 4 dozen chips.

Festive ice cubes! Drop a couple of cranberries and a sprig of mint into each section of an ice cube tray. Fill with distilled water for crystal-clear cubes and freeze.

Happy Time Sherbet Punch

Kathy Gideon
Corryton, TN

I have been making this delicious punch at Christmas for many years. It is almost like a dessert. The holidays wouldn't be the same without it!

2 6-oz. cans frozen lemonade concentrate	9 c. cold water
6-oz. can frozen orange juice concentrate	5 pts. pineapple sherbet
	1 qt. vanilla ice cream

In a large pitcher, combine frozen juices and water; mix well and refrigerate. This can be done the night before. At serving time, place sherbet and ice cream in a punch bowl, breaking into small pieces. Add juice mixture and stir, leaving some chunks of sherbet and ice cream. Makes 5 quarts.

I am going to be 63 this December, so this memory goes back lots of years. I had gone to a children's Christmas party with the neighbors. When we went home, I remember coming across the street and seeing the windows all foggy in the house so it blurred the Christmas tree lights. They looked so beautiful that way. I came into the house and the smell of cookies baking just overwhelmed me. Here was my mom making Christmas cookies for my whole class...not just one apiece, but enough for 3 or 4 apiece! They were all frosted and decorated, made with love. This memory has always been in my mind every Christmas since. Mom has been gone more than 20 years now. But the memory is fresh.

–Cheryl Hanley, Gerber, CA

Mushroom-Stuffed Chicken Pinwheels

Deanna Lyons
Columbus, OH

Rich and delicious. If you love mushrooms, you'll love this recipe. I serve this each year around the holidays. My family & friends can't get enough!

5 T. butter, divided
1/2 lb. mushrooms, chopped
salt and pepper to taste
1 c. seasoned dry bread crumbs, divided
1/2 t. nutmeg
6 boneless, skinless chicken breasts, cut in half lengthwise
3/4 c. whipping cream

Melt 4 tablespoons butter in a small skillet over medium heat. Sauté mushrooms until tender; season with salt and pepper. Remove from heat. Stir in 3/4 cup bread crumbs and nutmeg; set aside. Pound each chicken strip to 1/4-inch thick. Spoon mushroom mixture evenly over chicken strips. Roll up each strip and fasten with a wooden toothpick. Place in a lightly greased 13"x9" baking pan. Melt remaining butter and brush over rolled strips; sprinkle with remaining bread crumbs. Pour cream over all. Bake, uncovered, at 350 degrees for 30 minutes, or until golden and juices run clear when chicken is pierced. Makes 12 servings.

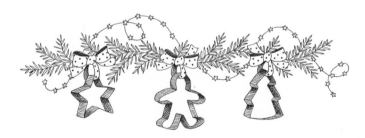

Feeling rushed at Christmas? Streamline your holiday plans... ask your family what traditions they most look forward to, including favorite cookies and other festive foods. Then you can focus on tried & true activities, freeing up time to try something new and meaningful to you.

Cheesy Crab-Stuffed Mushrooms
Susie Backus
Delaware, OH

These are so simple to make and a favorite at parties.
There are never any leftovers!

6-oz. can crabmeat, drained
    and flaked
1/2 c. butter, melted
1/2 c. Italian-seasoned dry
    bread crumbs
3/4 c. grated Parmesan cheese

3/4 c. shredded mozzarella
    cheese
3 cloves garlic, pressed
3/4 to 1 lb. whole mushrooms,
    stems removed
1/2 c. chilled butter, diced

In a bowl, combine all ingredients except mushrooms and chilled
butter. Mix well and set aside. Place mushroom caps in an ungreased
13"x9" baking pan. Spoon mixture into mushrooms. Add diced
butter to the pan, in between the mushrooms. Bake, uncovered,
at 375 degrees for 20 to 30 minutes, until bubbly and golden.
Makes about 10 servings.

Turn thrift-store holiday teacups into twinkly candles...
just fill with pine-scented wax chips and tuck in a wick.
Group together on a mirrored tray for extra sparkle.

Aunt Rita's Shrimp Dip

Lori Williams
Acton, ME

Every time I make this recipe, I think of my Aunt Rita and my grandmother too! They were sisters-in-law and they had so much fun together. This recipe is so easy because all of the ingredients are pantry staples. Whip it up whenever it's party time.

8-oz. pkg. cream cheese, softened	1/2 c. celery, finely chopped
1 T. mayonnaise	1/4 c. onion, finely chopped
1 t. catsup	4-1/4 oz. can tiny shrimp, drained
1 t. mustard	hearty crackers

In a bowl, blend together cream cheese, mayonnaise, catsup and mustard. Stir in celery and onion; gently fold in shrimp. Cover and chill for at least one hour. Serve with crackers. Serves 8.

Serve a variety of baby vegetables and sliced veggies on a platter for dipping. Tuck sprigs of fresh rosemary between the veggies for a holiday accent.

Hot Clam Dip

Denise Bliss
Milton, NH

*Our family has loved this warm yummy dip together
on a cold winter evening during family movie night.*

1 onion, chopped
1/2 c. butter, sliced
2 6-1/2 oz. cans chopped clams
1 t. lemon juice
1 c. seasoned dry bread crumbs

1/4 t. dried oregano
8-oz. pkg. shredded mozzarella
   cheese
snack crackers

In a saucepan over medium heat, sauté onion in butter until translucent. Add clams with juice and lemon juice; simmer over medium-low heat for 10 minutes. Remove from heat. Add bread crumbs and oregano; mix well. Stir in cheese. Spoon mixture into an ungreased 9" pie plate. Bake, uncovered, at 350 degrees for 30 minutes, or until bubbly and lightly golden. Serve warm with crackers. Makes 6 to 8 servings.

In Grandmother's day, Christmas gifts were so much simpler.
Recall those times with charming table favors. Fill brown
paper lunch sacks with a juicy orange, a popcorn ball, nuts and
old-fashioned hard candies. Tie with yarn and set one
at each place, or heap in a basket. So sweet!

Aloha Chicken Wings

Nancy Girard
Chesapeake, VA

These wings are delicious and will be a great addition to your next party!

3 lbs. chicken wings, separated
1 c. pineapple preserves
1/2 c. dry sherry or apple juice
1/2 c. frozen orange juice
    concentrate
1/2 c. soy sauce
1/2 c. brown sugar, packed
1/4 c. oil
1 t. garlic powder
1 t. ground ginger

Place wings in a large plastic zipping bag; set aside. In a bowl, combine remaining ingredients; stir until thoroughly combined. Pour mixture over wings in bag; seal. Squeeze bag to spread marinade over all parts of wings. Refrigerate for 6 hours to overnight, turning bag occasionally. Drain marinade into a saucepan; bring to a boil. Place wings on an aluminum foil-covered shallow baking pan. Pour one cup of marinade over wings; discard any remaining marinade. Bake, uncovered, at 350 degrees for one hour, turning occasionally, until wings are golden and juices run clear when pierced. Makes 12 to 15 servings.

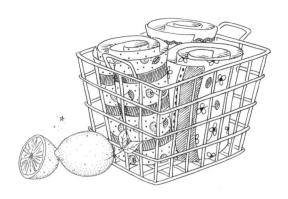

When serving saucy party foods like chicken wings and barbecue ribs, set out a basket of rolled-up fingertip towels, moistened with lemon-scented water and warmed briefly in the microwave. A thoughtful touch guests are sure to appreciate.

Festive Cranberry-Cheese Spread

Arlene Smulski
Lyons, IL

This cheery appetizer is perfect for parties during the holiday season. It has a very short prep time and both adults and kids will gobble it up.

8-oz. pkg. cream cheese, softened
1/2 c. sweetened dried cranberries, chopped
1/2 c. dried apricots, chopped

1/4 c. chopped walnuts
1 t. orange zest
assorted crackers or party rye bread

In a large bowl, combine all ingredients except crackers or bread. Beat until well blended. Cover and chill until serving time. Serve with crackers or party rye slices. Serves 8 to 10.

Cranberry Jezebel Sauce

Zoe Bennett
Columbia, SC

We love this sassy sauce with a holiday twist! Spoon it over cream cheese and serve with crackers for an easy appetizer.

1 c. water
1/2 c. sugar
1/2 c. brown sugar, packed

12-oz. pkg. fresh cranberries
3 T. prepared horseradish
1 T. Dijon mustard

Combine water and sugars in a saucepan. Stir well; bring to a boil over medium heat. Add cranberries. Return to a boil; cook for 10 minutes, stirring occasionally. Spoon into a bowl; cool to room temperature. Stir in horseradish and mustard; cover and chill. Makes about 2-1/2 cups.

Show off Christmas cards...attach them to a length of rick rack and hang on either side of a doorway.

Christmas Comfort Classics

Savory Steak Sliders

JoAnn

These delectable little sandwiches are sure to be a hit at your next party! Perfect for a casual Christmas dinner too.

1/2 c. balsamic vinegar
3 T. Worcestershire sauce
1 clove garlic, minced
1-1/2 lbs. beef top round steak

16 slider buns, split and warmed
Garnish: horseradish sauce,
  Dijon mustard

In a large plastic zipping bag, combine vinegar, Worcestershire sauce and garlic; squeeze bag to mix. Add steak to bag; turn to coat well. Seal bag and refrigerate for 4 to 6 hours, turning several times to coat steak. Preheat broiler to high. Remove steak from bag; discard marinade. Place steak on a lightly greased broiler pan; place pan 2 to 3 inches under broiler. Broil for 6 to 8 minutes on each side, until medium-rare. Remove from oven; let stand for 5 minutes. Thinly slice steak on the diagonal. Divide steak slices among bun bottoms; garnish as desired and add tops of buns. Makes 16 sliders.

Be sure to ask your kids about their favorite holiday foods as you plan for the season's occasions. You may find you have "traditions" in your own family that you weren't even aware of!

Betty Lou's Beer Sausage

Betty Lou Wright
Hendersonville, TN

You don't have to be a beer drinker to like this zippy recipe...I'm not! In fact, I first tasted it at a Sunday School party at least 25 years ago. It continues to be a must-have at New Year's and other special times during the year.

12-oz. can regular or
   non-alcoholic beer,
   room temperature
1/4 c. mustard
1/4 c. vinegar

2 T. prepared horseradish
1/4 c. brown sugar, packed
2 T. cornstarch
2 lbs. Kielbasa sausage, sliced
   into bite-size pieces

In a saucepan over low heat, mix all ingredients except sausage. Simmer until brown sugar is dissolved and mixture is thick and bubbly. Add sausage; warm through. May be served from a slow cooker set on low. Makes 8 to 10 servings.

Make a party tray of savory bite-size appetizer tarts...
so impressive-looking, yet guests will never suspect how easy
they are! Bake frozen mini phyllo shells according to package
directions, then spoon in a favorite creamy dip or spread.

Bread & Garlic Filling Appetizer

Janis Parr
Ontario, Canada

This savory cheese-filled loaf for dipping is a favorite
with everyone. I always make two to be sure there is enough!

1 loaf Italian bread
2 8-oz. pkgs. cream cheese, softened
1 c. mayonnaise
1/4 c. onion, chopped
1 clove garlic, minced
1 c. shredded Cheddar cheese
3/4 c. frozen spinach, thawed and drained well
5 slices bacon, crisply cooked and crumbled
Optional: tortilla chips, snack crackers

Cut off the top of bread; hollow out loaf to make a bread bowl. Set aside bread bowl, top and pulled-out bread pieces. In a bowl, combine cream cheese and mayonnaise; stir well to combine. Add onion, garlic, shredded cheese, spinach and bacon; blend well. Spoon filling into bread bowl; replace top. Wrap well in aluminum foil. Bake at 325 degrees for one hour. Serve hot with reserved bread pieces, or with tortilla chips or snack crackers. Makes 10 to 12 servings.

Wrap toss pillows in holiday fabric and tie with brightly
colored ribbons just like gift packages! Add a few stitches
or tiny safety pins to hold the ribbons in place.

Spinach & Artichoke Dip

Janice Ertola
Martinez, CA

This dip is always a favorite whenever I make it. It is delicious warm and even good cold! It is wonderful served with tortilla chips. I like to double it and bake it in a bread loaf pan.

14-oz. can artichokes, drained
  and chopped
10-oz. pkg. frozen chopped
  spinach, thawed and
  well drained
2 T. Italian-seasoned dry
  bread crumbs

1 c. mayonnaise
1/2 c. shredded Parmesan
  cheese
1/2 t. garlic, minced
1/2 t. pepper
tortilla chips

In a bowl, combine all ingredients except tortilla chips. Stir to mix well; spoon into a one-quart casserole dish. Bake at 400 degrees for 8 to 10 minutes, until hot and bubbly. Serve warm with tortilla chips. Makes 2 cups.

Legend has it that burning a bayberry candle on Christmas Eve brings good luck throughout the new year. Stack ribbon-tied bundles of sweetly scented candles in a basket near the front door...a pretty decoration that doubles as gifts for visitors.

Bacon-Wrapped Water Chestnuts

Krista Marshall
Fort Wayne, IN

My grandma taught me to make these little gems, and I couldn't believe how easy they were. They are always a hit at parties. I'm pretty sure the secret is in the sauce!

1 c. catsup
1 c. brown sugar, packed
1 lb. bacon, sliced into thirds

2 8-oz. cans whole water
  chestnuts, drained

In a small saucepan over low heat, combine catsup and brown sugar. Cook, stirring often, until brown sugar is dissolved and sauce is well combined. Meanwhile, wrap a piece of bacon around each water chestnut. Place in a lightly greased 8"x8" baking pan, seam-side down. Spoon sauce over top. Bake, covered, at 350 degrees for 45 minutes, until bacon is crisp and sauce is thickened slightly. Serves 10.

Bacon-Wrapped Dates

Claire Bertram
Lexington, KY

A very old-fashioned party treat...Grandma used to make these.

8-oz. pkg. Gorgonzola cheese,
  cut into small strips

10-oz. pkg. pitted whole dates
1 lb. bacon, sliced into thirds

Stuff a piece of cheese into each date; wrap with a piece of bacon. Fasten with a wooden toothpick. Place dates on a parchment paper-lined baking sheet. Bake, uncovered, at 375 degrees for 20 to 25 minutes, until bacon is crisp and golden. Drain on paper towels. Cool slightly before serving. Serves 8 to 10.

Add pizzazz to an appetizer tray... glue tiny, sparkly Christmas balls onto long toothpicks for serving.

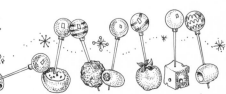

Tree Trimming
Open House

Easy Dipping Fondue

Gloria Morris
British Columbia, Canada

Our minister's wife served this at a New Year's Eve gathering. It is so good, you will definitely want to try it yourself! Serve, and wait for the oooh's and ahhh's.

18-oz. jar grape jelly
12-oz. bottle chili sauce
19-oz. can pineapple chunks,
 drained

2 lbs. mini smoked sausages,
 sliced if desired

In a saucepan over low heat, simmer jelly and chili sauce until blended, stirring often. Add pineapple and sausages; heat through. Makes 15 to 20 servings.

Beer Hot Dogs

Kimberly Peters
Lock Haven, PA

This is a Christmas tradition in our family. My mom serves these every year with our Christmas Eve dinner. If you'd like more sauce, combine equal parts of the sauce ingredients.

1 c. brown sugar, packed
1 c. catsup

1 c. beer or non-alcoholic beer
3 lbs. hot dogs, cut into thirds

Combine brown sugar, catsup and beer in a saucepan over low heat. Cook, stirring often, until brown sugar is dissolved. Pour over hot dogs in a 3 to 4-quart slow cooker; stir to coat. Cover and cook on low setting for 3 to 4 hours, until hot dogs are plump and well coated with sauce. Makes 15 servings.

Remembrance, like a candle,
burns brightest at Christmastime.

–Charles Dickens

Spicy Snack Mix

Lauren Stege
Saint Charles, MO

My grandmother brings this snack mix to every gathering and people always beg her for the recipe. It's so much better than any bagged mix you can buy at the grocery store!

6 c. bite-size crispy corn cereal
    squares
6 c. bite-size crispy rice cereal
    squares
6 c. bite-size crispy wheat cereal
    squares
2 c. mini twist or stick pretzels
2 c. mixed nuts
1/2 c. butter, melted

2 T. Worcestershire sauce
4 to 6 t. hot pepper sauce
1 T. garlic salt
1 T. onion salt
1 T. celery salt
1 T. cayenne pepper
1 T. allspice
1 T. flavor enhancer
1-1/2 t. seasoning salt

Mix together cereal, pretzels and nuts in an ungreased large roasting pan; set aside. In a bowl, stir together remaining ingredients. Add butter mixture to cereal mixture, stirring quickly to coat well. Bake, uncovered, at 250 degrees for one hour, stirring every 15 minutes. Pour mixture out onto paper towels to drain. When completely cooled, store in an airtight container. Makes 22 cups.

Serve party popcorn or snack mix in a big bowl along with a scoop. A stack of lunch-size paper bags nearby will make it easy for everyone to help themselves.

Paulette's Spiced Peanuts

Paulette Alexander
Newfoundland, Canada

I came across this tasty recipe a few years ago, and tweaked it
to my own liking. Everybody loves it at Christmastime!

2 c. unsalted peanuts
2 t. olive oil
2 t. chili powder
1/4 t. cayenne pepper

1/4 t. red pepper flakes
1/4 t. garlic powder
celery salt to taste

In a bowl, combine all ingredients except celery salt; toss to coat peanuts well. Spread peanuts on an ungreased baking sheet. Bake at 300 degrees for 20 minutes, stirring after 10 and 15 minutes. Sprinkle with celery salt. Pour peanuts onto paper towels; rub gently and sprinkle with celery salt again. Cool; store in a covered container. Makes 2 cups.

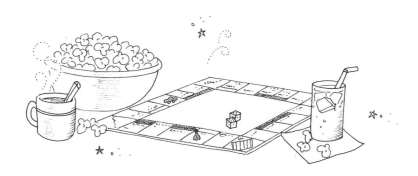

Stay in on a snowy night...fill the table with lots of
tasty snacks and pull out a board game or two.
What fun for the entire family!

Cannoli Dip

Audra Vanhorn-Sorey
Columbia, NC

A fun spin on a sweet Italian favorite!

8-oz. pkg. cream cheese,
  softened
1/2 c. butter, softened
3/4 c. powdered sugar
1/2 t. vanilla extract

1 c. mini semi-sweet chocolate
  chips
plain or cinnamon graham
  crackers or vanilla wafers

In a large bowl, combine cream cheese and butter; blend well. Add powdered sugar; stir well until smooth. Stir in vanilla; fold in chocolate chips. Cover and chill, if not serving immediately. Serve with graham crackers or vanilla wafers. Makes 10 servings.

Setting up a holiday party? Serve easy-to-handle foods and beverages at tables in several different rooms around the house. Guests will be able to snack and mingle easily.

Andrea's Choco-Chip Cookie Dough Dip

Andrea Heyart
Savannah, TX

This dip tastes so much like actual chocolate chip cookie dough you'll be tempted to try and bake it. Always a hit at parties. Make sure to save some for the hostess...it disappears in a flash!

8-oz. pkg. cream cheese, softened
1/2 c. butter, softened
1-1/4 c. brown sugar, packed
1/2 c. powdered sugar
2 T. all-purpose flour
1/4 t. salt
1-1/2 t. vanilla extract
3/4 c. mini semi-sweet chocolate chips
graham cracker sticks or vanilla wafers

In a large bowl, combine cream cheese and butter; mix well. With a electric mixer on low speed, gradually beat in sugars. Add flour, salt and vanilla; continue beating until smooth and creamy. Gently fold in chocolate chips with a spoon. Cover and chill. Serve with graham cracker sticks or vanilla wafers. Makes 2 cups.

Snap a photo of your family in the same place and same position each year. It will be a sweet reminder of how the kids have grown!

Celebration Party Mix

Frances Click
Hernando Beach, FL

We serve this snack mix on many occasions. My husband loves it and is always looking for a reason to celebrate! Just change the color of the candy-coated milk chocolate pieces to suit the occasion.

2 c. bite-size crispy corn cereal squares
2 c. mini pretzels

1 c. cocktail peanuts
1 c. candy-coated chocolates
12-oz. pkg white chocolate chips

In a large bowl, combine all ingredients except chocolate chips; toss to mix and set aside. Place chocolate chips in a microwave-safe bowl. Microwave for one minute; stir. Microwave again as needed, 15 seconds at a time, until melted. Stir chocolate until smooth. Pour over cereal mixture; toss to coat. Immediately pour onto wax paper lined baking sheets; spread out. Let stand until chocolate is set, about 20 minutes. Break into pieces. Store in an airtight container. Makes about 8 cups.

When I was in kindergarten, we had a Christmas program at school. We sat up front on the gym floor. Santa came in and greeted all of us children. Then he asked if anyone knew how to sing "Rudolph, the Red-Nosed Reindeer." I raised my hand and excitedly said, "I do, Santa, I do!" So he had me get up and sing it. Then he asked if anyone knew "Jingle Bells." Of course, since I loved Santa, I said "I do, Santa, I do." I think my mother was mortified...ha! However, he chose someone else that time. My family never let me live that one down. Every Christmas I was reminded of my "Rudolph, the Red-Nosed Reindeer" escapade, even when I was grown and married!

–Gert Stevens, Sioux City, IA

Candied Pecans

Ann Mathis
Biscoe, AR

We have huge pecan trees in our yard that were planted by my father, grandfather and great-grandfather. Some years, they yield so many pecans we give them away! A rare treat for some people. But we believe in sharing the bounty.

2-3/4 c. pecan halves
2 T. butter, softened and divided
1 c. sugar
1/2 c. water

1/2 t. salt
1/2 t. cinnamon
1 t. vanilla extract

Place pecans in an ungreased shallow baking pan. Bake at 250 degrees for 10 minutes, or until warmed. Coat a 15"x10" jelly-roll pan with one tablespoon butter; set aside. Grease the sides of a large heavy saucepan with remaining butter; add sugar, water, salt and cinnamon. Cook and stir over low heat until sugar dissolves. Continue cooking and stirring until mixture comes to a boil. Cover and cook for 2 minutes to dissolve sugar crystals. Cook without stirring until mixture reaches the soft-ball stage, or 234 to 243 degrees on a candy thermometer. Remove from heat; stir in vanilla. Add warm pecans; stir until evenly coated. Spread onto buttered pan; let cool. Stir in a covered container. Makes 3 cups.

Spread out cotton batting as a snowy setting for tiny vintage houses and reindeer or snowman figures...what a sweet centerpiece! Add a dash of mica flakes for icy sparkle.

Holiday Wassail

Pamela Bennett
Whittier, CA

More than 20 years ago, I received this recipe from a stranger at the grocery store. I had asked her an opinion on an item I was considering for my annual Christmas party. She proceeded to share this recipe with me. I was so excited to try it. I made it for my party and it was a huge hit...so tasty! I've made it many times since, usually adding the wine. A favorite every time. And there's always requests for the recipe!

1 gal. apple cider
1 c. light brown sugar, packed
6-oz. can frozen lemonade
    concentrate
6-oz. can frozen orange juice
    concentrate

12 whole cloves
6 whole allspice
4 4-inch cinnamon sticks
1 t. ground nutmeg
Optional: 750-ml. bottle
    port wine

Combine cider, brown sugar and juices in a large pot over medium heat; stir well. Divide spices evenly between 2 empty family-size tea bags or small muslin spice bags; tie closed with thread. Add spice bags to pot with cider mixture; simmer about 20 minutes. Add a little water if liquid seems too thick. Transfer to a 6 to 7-quart slow cooker. Add wine if using; cover and warm through on low setting. Keep warm on low setting for serving. Serves 15.

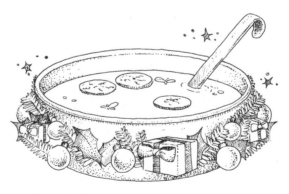

Nestle a sparkling punch bowl in the prettiest wreath. Wrap mini gift boxes in scraps of gift wrap and hot-glue then to a wreath form, then tuck in tiny, shiny ornament balls between the boxes.

Snowy
Day
Soups & Breads

Creamy Chicken-Rice Soup

Amanda Hettinger
Kirkwood, MO

I make this hearty soup on Christmas Eve to enjoy with crusty rolls while watching our favorite Christmas movie. A deli roast chicken makes it simple and delicious. When I think of this soup, I think of comfort and joyful memories...it really is a wonderful life!

8 c. chicken broth
1/2 c. onion, finely chopped
1 cube chicken bouillon
1/4 t. garlic powder
1/4 t. dried thyme
1/4 c. butter, sliced
1/4 c. all-purpose flour

10-3/4 oz. can low-sodium
  cream of chicken soup
1/2 c. white wine or chicken
  broth
3 c. cooked chicken breast,
  shredded
4 c. cooked wild rice

Combine broth, onion, bouillon and seasonings in a soup pot over high heat. Bring to a boil; reduce heat to medium-low and simmer for 30 minutes. In another large soup pot, melt butter over medium heat. Whisk in flour until smooth; cook for 2 to 3 minutes, until mixture loses its flour taste. Gradually whisk in hot broth mixture. Bring to a boil; cook and stir for 2 minutes, or until slightly thickened. Whisk in canned soup and wine or broth. Stir in chicken and cooked rice; heat through. Serves 8.

A charming welcome! Fill Victorian-style paper cones
with old-fashioned hard candies and tiny toys.
Hang from chair backs with ribbons.

Beckie's Down-Home Potato Soup

Beckie Apple
Grannis, AR

This potato soup is my favorite to warm the body & soul. I grew up on savory stews & soups and am fortunate that my husband and son also love a warm bowl of soup with a big square of cornbread.

6 potatoes, peeled and cut into
   2-inch cubes
2 onions, coarsely chopped
3 carrots, peeled and diced
2 stalks celery, sliced
2 14-oz. cans chicken broth
3 c. hot water
1 t. salt

1 t. pepper
1/2 t. garlic powder
6-oz. can chunk ham, flaked
2 c. milk
2 c. shredded Cheddar cheese,
   or 6 to 8 slices American
   cheese

In a large soup pot over medium heat, combine vegetables, broth, water and seasonings. Bring to a boil; reduce heat to medium-low and simmer until vegetables are tender, 15 to 20 minutes. Do not drain. Mash potatoes in the pot, using a potato masher. Add ham, milk and cheese. Continue to simmer over low heat for about 10 minutes. Season with additional salt, pepper or garlic powder, if desired. Serves 8 to 10.

Host a caroling party...gather up friends and serenade the neighbors! Back home, have slow cookers waiting, filled with yummy soup and a hot beverage ready to warm everyone up. Add a platter of cookies for dessert and you're done!

Homemade Chicken Noodle Soup

Michelle Kiser
Nixa, MO

This is one of my family's most-requested wintertime meals. It not only warms them up, but fills the house with a delicious smell!

16-oz. pkg. frozen egg noodles, uncooked
1 c. carrot, peeled and chopped
1/2 c. onion, chopped
1/2 c. celery, chopped
5 cubes chicken bouillon
3 bay leaves
1 t. garlic powder

1/2 t. dried thyme
salt and pepper to taste
3 chicken breasts, cooked and shredded
1 c. milk
1/2 c. frozen peas
Garnish: shredded cheese, saltine crackers

Cook noodles according to package directions; drain. Meanwhile, in a separate stockpot, combine carrot, onion and celery. Barely cover with water. Add bouillon cubes and seasonings. Bring to a boil over medium-high heat. Reduce heat to low; simmer until vegetables are tender, about 15 minutes. Do not drain. Add chicken, cooked egg noodles and enough water to cover all ingredients. Bring water back to a boil; reduce heat to low. Simmer for about 30 minutes, stirring occasionally. Add milk and frozen peas during the last 5 to 10 minutes. Remove bay leaves before serving. Serve with shredded cheese and crackers. Makes 12 servings.

For juicy, tender cooked chicken, try poaching. Cover boneless, skinless chicken breasts with water in a saucepan. Bring to a boil, then turn down the heat, cover and simmer over low heat for 10 to 12 minutes. Chicken is done when it is no longer pink in the center.

Zucchini Pecan Bread

Deborah Douma
Pensacola, FL

This recipe has been in my recipe box since 1978. It first came from a neighbor while we were living in married student housing. It is delicious toasted! Also makes great muffins.

2 c. zucchini, grated
3 eggs
1 c. canola oil
2 c. brown sugar, packed
1 T. vanilla extract
3 c. all-purpose flour

1 t. salt
1 t. baking powder
1 t. baking soda
1 T. cinnamon
1 c. chopped pecans

Squeeze out excess liquid from zucchini; set aside. In a large bowl, beat together eggs, oil, brown sugar and vanilla; stir in zucchini. Add remaining ingredients; stir until well moistened. Divide batter between 2 lightly greased 9"x5" loaf pans. Bake at 325 degrees for 55 to 60 minutes, until a toothpick comes out clean. Let cool 10 minutes; turn loaves out of pans and cool on wire racks before slicing. Makes 2 loaves.

My baby sister Gerry wanted a bike for Christmas. My dad put the bike together, but hid it outside. He took the instructions for putting the bike together and wrapped them in a matchbox. He took that box and put it in another slightly larger box and kept doing that until he had a huge box. My sister was so excited when she saw this huge box under the tree. She unwrapped it, and imagine her surprise when the box was empty. She found the next box and kept going until she got to the matchbox. She looked at the pictures for the bike and was so upset that the bike wasn't there. My dad told her to look outside... and there was the bike! My dad laughed so hard at my poor confused sister but I loved this Christmas best of all!

–Melissa Austin, Thomasville, NC

Brunswick Stew

Christy Bonner
Bessemer, AL

I love Brunswick stew! After much trial & error, I've found the right combination suited to my taste. This is a true crowd-pleaser and always keeps 'em coming back for more. One Christmas with my grandmother's family, everyone scraped the pot clean! They all left with a copy of this recipe in hand, they loved it so much.

4-lb. Boston butt pork roast
salt and pepper to taste
4 chicken breasts
10 c. water
3 potatoes, peeled and chopped
1 onion, chopped
28-oz. can diced tomatoes
26-oz. bottle catsup

2 15-1/4 oz. cans corn, drained
2 14-3/4 oz. cans creamed corn
1/2 c. Worcestershire sauce
1/4 c. butter
2 T. smoke-flavored cooking
 sauce
2 t. hot pepper sauce, or to taste

Place pork roast fat-side up in a 6-quart slow cooker. Season well with salt and pepper. Cover and cook on low setting for 8 to 10 hours, until very tender. Drain and cool; shred with 2 forks. This step may be done a day ahead. Next, in a large stockpot, combine chicken and water. Bring to a boil over medium-high heat. Reduce heat to low; cover and simmer for 35 to 40 minutes. Remove chicken to a plate and cool, reserving broth in stockpot. Cut chicken into bite-size pieces, discarding bones and skin; set aside. Add potatoes and onion to reserved broth. Bring to a boil; reduce heat and cook until vegetables are tender, about 25 minutes. Stir in pork, chicken, tomatoes with juice and remaining ingredients. Simmer, uncovered, over low heat for one hour, stirring occasionally. Makes 15 servings.

Why not get out Grandma's soup tureen set for cozy soup dinners? The ladle makes serving easy and the lid keeps soup piping hot and steamy.

Snowy Day
Soups & Breads

Lela's Beef & Vegetable Soup

Faye Coggins
Wilson, NC

How many ways can you fix soup...a lot! But I have never had a bowl of soup as good as my mother-in-law made. I have worked in a busy medical office for 45 years. The days could be long and to go home and fix supper was often an effort. When Mrs. Coggins would call around 4 p.m. and say, "When you get off, come by, I've got a pot of soup for your supper," it always made my day! I was thrilled. Her soup was always thick and hearty. The more you warmed it up, the better it got. I have never been able to make it just like she did, but this slow-cooker recipe is pretty good too.

1/2 lb. lean ground beef
14-1/2 oz. can diced tomatoes
10-1/2 oz. can beef broth
16-oz. can diced potatoes, drained
15-1/4 oz. can garden peas, drained

15-oz. can shoepeg corn, drained
15-oz. can butter beans, drained
14-1/2 oz. can cut green beans, drained
48-oz. can tomato juice
4 to 5 T. sugar

Brown beef in a skillet over medium heat. Drain; transfer to a 6-quart slow cooker. Add tomatoes with juice, broth, vegetables and enough tomato juice to cover vegetables and make a nice soup consistency. Stir well. Stir in sugar as desired to cut tartness of tomatoes. Cover and cook on low setting for 5 hours, stirring every 30 minutes. Makes 8 servings.

Bundle up the kids and take a ride to enjoy all the holiday lights... the kids can even wear their pajamas! Wrap up in cozy blankets, sing carols and enjoy a fun-filled evening together.

French Onion Soup

Jennifer Manwaring
Salt Lake City, UT

This is definitely a comfort food. So delicious, and when served in individual crocks, you can't help but feel the holiday spirit!

1/2 c. butter
6 onions, thinly sliced and
    divided
1 T. salt, divided
4 T. all-purpose flour, divided
8 c. beef broth
3/4 c. apple cider
1 t. pepper
8 slices crusty French bread
olive oil to taste
1 c. Gruyère cheese, grated

Melt butter in a large skillet over medium heat. Layer half of onions in skillet; sprinkle evenly with half of salt and half of flour. Repeat layering; do not stir. Cook without stirring for about 15 minutes; stir. Continue cooking, stirring occasionally, for 4 minutes, or until onions are soft, deeply golden and have cooked down to about 2 cups. Add broth, cider and pepper to skillet. Reduce heat to medium-low; simmer for 15 minutes. Meanwhile, place an oven rack in the top 1/3 of the oven; preheat broiler. Place bread slices on a baking sheet; drizzle with oil. Broil for one minute per side. Ladle soup into 8 oven-safe soup crocks. Top each crock with a toasted bread slice and 2 tablespoons cheese. Place crocks on baking sheet. Broil until cheese is bubbly and golden, about 2 minutes. Makes 8 servings.

Sing we all merrily, Christmas is here,
The day we love best of all days in the year.

–Old English Poem

Cheesy Potato Soup

Rebecca Etling
Blairsville, PA

This slow-cooker soup is delicious, quick & easy!

1 red onion, finely chopped
1 to 2 cloves garlic, minced
2 T. butter
30-oz. pkg. frozen diced
   potatoes
14-1/2 oz. can chicken broth
23-oz. can cream of mushroom
   or chicken soup
10-3/4 oz. can cream of celery
   soup

1 lb. bacon, crisply cooked,
   crumbled and divided
8-oz. pkg. cream cheese,
   softened and cubed
1 to 1-1/2 c. shredded Cheddar
   cheese
salt and pepper to taste

In a skillet over medium heat, cook onion and garlic in butter until tender. Transfer onion mixture to a 5 to 6-quart slow cooker. Add potatoes, broth, soups and half of the crumbled bacon. Cover and cook on low setting for 6 to 7 hours. Stir in cheeses; cover and cook for a few more minutes, until melted. Season with salt and pepper as desired. Serve soup topped with remaining bacon. Makes 8 to 10 servings.

"I love my grandparents because..." Have little ones write down all the reasons they love their grandparents and present the list at Christmas. Handwritten on special paper and framed, it'll make a truly meaningful gift.

Hearty Sausage-White Bean & Spinach Soup

Tyson Ann Trecannelli
Gettysburg, PA

A wonderfully flavorful, healthy, hearty soup that's pure comfort food. Sure to please and they'll come back for more. Serve with some good crusty bread.

2 lbs. ground pork country
  or Italian sausage
2 T. olive oil
2 to 3 leeks, chopped
2 to 3 carrots, peeled and
  chopped
2 to 3 stalks celery, chopped
2 to 3 cloves garlic, chopped

1 t. salt
3 32-oz. containers chicken
  broth
3 15-oz. cans navy beans,
  drained and rinsed
3 to 4 c. baby spinach
salt and pepper to taste

In a large stockpot over medium heat, crumble and brown sausage, stirring often; drain and set aside in a bowl. Add oil, vegetables and garlic to same stockpot; sprinkle with salt. Sauté until leeks are soft and translucent, scraping any bits of sausage from bottom of pot. Stir in broth; return sausage to stockpot. Bring to a boil; reduce heat to low. Simmer for one hour, stirring occasionally. Skim off any fat as it rises to the top. Stir in beans; simmer for another 20 minutes. Stir in spinach, a handful at a time, until wilted into soup. Season with salt and pepper. Makes 8 to 10 servings.

Try a jar of chicken or beef soup base next time you cook up a pot of soup. It's a pastelike product that adds extra-rich homemade flavor to recipes. Easy to store too...one jar in the fridge can replace a whole shelf of canned broth.

Washington Chowder

Diane Fliss
Arvada, CO

This is a recipe my mother always made for Friday night suppers when I was a child. It was one of my favorites then and it still is today. It's one of my comfort foods.

2 potatoes, peeled and cubed
1 onion, diced
1-1/2 c. water
1 T. margarine
salt to taste

1 c. canned creamed corn
1 c. canned whole tomatoes,
  mashed
2 c. evaporated milk

In a large saucepan over medium-high heat, combine potatoes, onion and water. Cook for 15 to 20 minutes, until potatoes are tender; do not drain. Add margarine, salt, corn and tomatoes. Bring to a boil; remove from heat. Add evaporated milk. Serves 8.

Macaroni & Tomato Soup

Kristie Bouldin
Trinity, NC

I love to make this quick & easy soup when I want some comfort food. I first tasted this delicious soup in my grandmother's kitchen over 50 years ago. She lived 75 miles away and I did not get to eat in her kitchen very often. Several years ago I was visiting with my aunt, who went into the kitchen to whip up something fast. It was the same soup! These ingredients are almost always on hand.

1 c. elbow macaroni, uncooked
2 c. canned whole tomatoes or
  tomato juice
6 T. margarine

salt and pepper to taste
2 T. onion, diced
2 T. green pepper, diced

Cook macaroni according to package directions, until nearly tender; drain well. Add remaining ingredients; stir. Continue to cook over medium-low heat until vegetables are tender. Serves 2.

Mom's Cinnamon Biscuits

Paula Marchesi
Lenhartsville, PA

You'll love these delicious cinnamon biscuits! I serve them to my family every Sunday after church. Our family would gather around the table to eat, talk and laugh for hours, and these biscuits were always a hit. I now make 3 batches, especially since our family keeps growing every couple of years.

2 c. all-purpose flour
1 T. baking powder
1 t. cinnamon
1 t. salt
1/3 c. shortening

2/3 c. 2% milk
1/2 t. vanilla extract
1 egg, lightly beaten
Optional: cinnamon-sugar

In a large bowl, whisk together flour, baking powder, cinnamon and salt. Cut in shortening until mixture resembles coarse crumbs. Add milk and vanilla; stir just until moistened. Turn dough out onto a lightly floured surface; knead gently 8 to 10 times. Pat dough into a 10-inch by 4-inch rectangle. Cut rectangle lengthwise in half; cut crosswise to make 10 squares. Place squares one inch apart on an ungreased baking sheet. Brush tops with egg. If desired, sprinkle with cinnamon-sugar. Bake at 450 degrees for 8 to 10 minutes, until golden. Serve warm. Makes 10 biscuits.

Early in the holiday season, it's good to check your spice rack for freshness. Crush a pinch of each spice...if it has a fresh, zingy scent, it's still good. Toss out any old-smelling spices and stock up on ones you've used up during the year.

Adena's Refrigerator Bran Muffins

Sandra Smith
Quartz Hill, CA

Adena is the daughter of my best friend, and once when my brother & I were traveling, we stopped to spend the night with Adena & her family. The next morning, we awoke to the smell of something good baking in the oven. The muffins were wonderful and I asked for the recipe...here it is! That was over 20 years ago. I have played around with this recipe for years, depending on what I have in the pantry. You can add almost any kind of dried fruit to it. It's really flexible.

3 c. sugar
5 c. all-purpose flour
5 t. baking soda
2 t. salt
15-oz. pkg. bran & raisin cereal

4 c. buttermilk
4 eggs, beaten
1 c. oil
Optional: 2 c. chopped walnuts
    or pecans

Combine sugar, flour, baking soda, salt and cereal in a very large bowl; mix well. Add buttermilk, eggs, oil and nuts, if desired; stir well. Spoon batter into greased muffin cups, filling 2/3 full. Bake at 400 degrees for 15 minutes. Batter may be stored in a large plastic container in the refrigerator and baked as desired; do not stir the batter as you use it. Batter will keep up to 2 weeks. Makes 15 to 20 muffins.

Keep fresh-baked rolls hot alongside servings of soup. Before arranging rolls in a bread basket, place a terra-cotta warming tile in the bottom and line with a tea towel.

Sir Feeds-a-Lot Stew

KellyJean Gettelfinger
Sellersburg, IN

I make this slow-cooker stew for friends who are in need, knowing they will have many loved ones dropping in to visit them. This stew literally "feeds a lot" of tummies, thus its name. Everyone is always amazed to learn the stew's ingredients after they've tasted and enjoyed its hearty flavor.

2 10-3/4 oz. cans bean & bacon
   soup
2-1/2 c. water
3 potatoes, peeled and cubed
3 stalks celery, diced

3 carrots, peeled and thinly
   sliced
1 lb. smoked pork sausage,
   thickly sliced

Add canned soup to a 4 to 5-quart slow cooker. Gradually add water to slow cooker, stirring well after each addition until smooth. Add vegetables; mix well. Add sausage; mix well. Cover and cook on high setting for 8 to 9 hours, until vegetables are very soft. The longer this stew cooks, the better it tastes. Makes 12 servings.

Have the kids build a snowman at an older neighbor's house
while she's out shopping...won't she'll be delighted!

Old Shaker Herb Soup

Marcia Shaffer
Conneaut Lake, PA

This soup from the Shakers in Pittsburgh was used in all of their communities as a curative for illness. It's very good. I always keep some frozen in small portions to serve with toast, as needed.

2 T. butter, sliced
1/2 t. dried thyme
1/2 t. dried marjoram
8 c. chicken broth
3 ripe tomatoes, chopped,
    or 15-oz. can diced tomatoes

1/2 c. celery, diced
1/2 c. carrot, peeled and diced
1/2 c. onion, diced
1 clove garlic, minced
1 t. sugar
1 t. salt

Melt butter in a saucepan over low heat. Add herbs; simmer for 3 to 5 minutes. Transfer to a 4-quart slow cooker; add remaining ingredients. Cover and cook on low setting for 8 hours. Makes 8 to 10 servings.

Cure-All Chicken Soup

Michelle Powell
Valley, AL

This simple soup clears your sniffles and soothes your heart as it tickles your tastebuds!

4 chicken breasts
12 c. water
2 15-oz. cans diced tomatoes
    with green chiles

2 10-oz. pkgs. frozen creamed
    corn, thawed
1 c. milk
salt and pepper to taste

In a stockpot, combine chicken and water. Simmer over medium-low heat until chicken is tender. Remove chicken to a plate, reserving broth in pot. Add tomatoes with juice and corn to reserved broth. Dice chicken and add to broth, discarding skin and bones. Simmer over low heat for 2 hours. Stir in milk without boiling; season with salt and pepper. Makes 10 servings.

Filipino Pork & Vegetable Stew
Indai Rowland
Pryor, OK

I was born and raised in the Philippines. This is a soup my mother made when I was growing up. My little son loves anything made with tomato sauce, so I decided to add tomato sauce to this recipe in hopes he would like it. It is his favorite! It tastes even better heated up the second day.

3 T. oil
1 onion, chopped
3 to 4 carrots, peeled and sliced
4 cloves garlic, minced
3/4 lb. boneless pork ribs, cubed
   and most of fat trimmed
1 c. fresh or frozen green beans,
   cut in bite-size pieces

15-oz. can tomato sauce
5 to 6 c. water
1 bunch kale, coarsely chopped
   and center stalk removed
1 lb. sliced mushrooms
salt and pepper to taste
Optional: cooked rice

Heat oil in a Dutch oven over medium heat. Add onion, carrots and garlic; sauté until carrots are tender-crisp. Add pork cubes; cook on all sides until no longer pink on the outside. Stir in green beans, tomato sauce and enough water to completely cover the ingredients. Bring to a boil; reduce heat to medium-low. Cover and simmer for one hour. Stir in kale and mushrooms. Add remaining water if a thinner consistency is desired. Simmer for 15 minutes. Serve over cooked rice, if desired. Makes 8 servings.

Tie different lengths of ribbon to Christmas cookie cutters
and hang them from a curtain rod...just the
right touch for the kitchen window.

Chicken & Sweet Potato Stew

Dale Duncan
Waterloo, IA

*My family just loves comforting stews in chilly weather,
and I love saving time with my slow cooker. This recipe is just
a little different from the usual beef & potato stew!*

2-1/2 lbs. chicken thighs
4 c. sweet potatoes, peeled and
    cut into 2-inch cubes
2 c. sliced mushrooms
1 c. red onion, diced
4 cloves garlic, minced

1/2 c. dry white wine or chicken
    broth
1/2 t. dried rosemary
1/4 t. salt
1/4 t. pepper
1 c. frozen baby peas

Pull off chicken skin with a paper towel and discard; set chicken aside.
In a 5-quart slow cooker, layer sweet potatoes, chicken, mushrooms,
onion and garlic. Drizzle with wine or broth; sprinkle with seasonings.
Cover and cook on low setting for 6 to 8 hours. About 30 minutes
before serving, place frozen peas on top; cover and finish cooking. To
serve, place chicken and sweet potatoes on a platter. Pour cooking
juices into a dish; serve on the side. Serves 6.

Share a potted rosemary herb plant with friends. As a
symbol of remembrance, it's a sweet way of letting
them know you care.

Homestyle Beef Stew

Patty Fletcher-Cotronea
Rome, NY

This is a great slow-cooker recipe for a weeknight or a weekend.
Perfect with dumplings or a crusty loaf of bread.

2 to 2-1/2 lbs. stew beef cubes
1/4 c. all-purpose flour
1 t. paprika
1/4 t. salt
1/2 t. pepper
1 onion, chopped

3 potatoes, peeled and diced
4 to 5 carrots, peeled and sliced
2 to 3 stalks celery, diced
1-1/2 to 2 c. beef broth
1 t. Worcestershire sauce

Place beef cubes in a large plastic zipping bag. Add flour, paprika, salt
and pepper; seal bag and shake until beef is well coated. Add beef to a
5-quart slow cooker; sprinkle in any flour remaining in bag. Top with
vegetables; add beef and Worcestershire sauce. Stir gently. Cover and
cook on low setting for 10 to 12 hours, or on high setting for 4 to
6 hours, until beef and vegetables are tender. Makes 6 to 7 servings.

When my niece Ashley was five years old, she decided Santa needed
real food instead of just cookies. When it came time for her to go to
bed that Christmas Eve, her mom told her to get the milk and cookies
for Santa. She looked at her mom and said, "No, I am going to make
him a bologna sandwich." Her mom laughed and said, "OK, but why
the change?" Ashley looked at her with a straight face and said he
really needed something with a little substance to it instead of all
those cookies, "so he is getting sweet tea and a bologna sandwich."
That became the tradition from that Christmas Eve until now.
Southern traditions must live on!

–Sophia Collins, Okeechobee, FL

Cloverleaf Tater Rolls

Linda Rich
Bean Station, TN

My mother and her sisters all made yeast rolls often. This recipe was their favorite. Every time we had a family gathering, you could count on these rolls being there. They take some time to make, but are worth the effort. The leftover rolls are great if reheated.

1 c. mashed potatoes
2/3 c. shortening
1/3 c. sugar
1-1/2 t. salt
2 eggs, beaten
1 env. active dry yeast

1/2 c. warm water, 110 to
    115 degrees
1 c. warm milk, 110 to
    115 degrees
6 to 8 c. all-purpose flour
1/2 c. butter, melted

Warm potatoes in a microwave-safe dish; add potatoes to a large bowl. Add shortening, sugar, salt and eggs; mix well and set aside. In a cup, dissolve yeast in warm water; add warm milk. Add yeast mixture to potato mixture; mix well and stir in enough flour to make a stiff dough. Knead dough well on a floured surface. Place dough in a greased large bowl; cover with a tea towel and let rise in a warm place until double in bulk, about 2 to 3 hours. Knead dough slightly; brush top with melted butter. At this point, dough may be covered and refrigerated, then baked later. Shape dough into 36 small balls. Place 3 balls in each of 12 greased muffin cups. Cover and let rise until double in bulk, about 2 to 3 hours. Bake at 400 degrees for 15 to 20 minutes, until golden. Makes one dozen.

Many hands make light work, so why not invite friends to a wrapping bee? Everyone brings their gifts, tags, tape and ribbons, while you provide light refreshments. With everyone helping each other, all the gifts will be wrapped in a twinkling!

Easy Creamy Chicken Soup

Arden Regnier
East Moriches, NY

When the grandchildren visited and wanted a quick lunch on a cold day, I whipped this up with leftover noodles and roast chicken. For dinner, serve with a green salad and hot biscuits.

12-oz. pkg. fine egg noodles, divided and uncooked
1/4 c. onion, finely diced
2 carrots, peeled and finely diced
2 stalks celery, finely diced
2 T. oil
salt and pepper to taste

2 10-3/4 oz. cans cream of chicken soup
2 14-oz. cans chicken broth
1 cooked chicken breast, shredded
10-oz. pkg. frozen peas, thawed
salt and pepper to taste

Divide noodles in half; reserve half of noodles for use in another recipe. Cook remaining noodles according to package directions; drain. Meanwhile, in a soup pot, sauté onion, carrot and celery in oil until tender. Drain; season with salt and pepper. Reduce heat to low. Add canned soup and broth; whisk together and bring to a simmer. Stir in shredded chicken, cooked noodles and frozen peas. Simmer until heated through and peas are cooked. Makes 6 servings.

Give a gift card, plus a little extra! Cut a card-sized pocket from felt. Stitch or hot glue it to the front of a Christmas stocking to form a pocket for the gift card. Slip a little homemade gift into the stocking to go with the card.

Cincinnati Chicken Corn Chowder

Jayne Homsher
Cincinnati, OH

This soup is a tradition for the coldest of days in the wintertime to eat with family members. We make homemade garlic bread and also have a side of macaroni & cheese with this meal. I can assure you that no leftovers will be left to clean up. Even our dogs love the smell of this chowder when I am stirring this chowder on the stove... tails a-wagging!

3 potatoes, peeled and diced
1/4 c. butter
1 onion, chopped
3 T. all-purpose flour
32-oz. container chicken broth
2 smoked or cooked chicken
    breasts, diced

16-oz. pkg. frozen corn,
    thawed
4 c. light cream
1/2 t. dill weed
salt and pepper to taste

Place potatoes in a saucepan; cover with water. Bring to a boil over medium-high heat. Reduce heat to medium-low; cover and simmer until tender, about 20 minutes. Drain; allow potatoes to steam-dry in pan for one to 2 minutes. Meanwhile, melt butter in a soup pot over medium heat; cook onion until translucent, about 8 minutes. Sprinkle flour over onion mixture; cook, stirring constantly, until a paste forms. Cook for about one minute; whisk in broth. Add potatoes, chicken and corn. Cook and stir until mixture comes to a low boil and thickens, about 5 minutes. With a potato masher, slightly mash potatoes. Add cream and dill; return soup to a simmer. Cook without boiling for 5 minutes, stirring constantly. Season with salt and pepper.
Makes 8 servings.

Evaporated milk can be substituted whenever a recipe calls for cream or regular milk. Keep a few cans in the pantry for rich, creamy soups...and no last-minute trips to the store in icy weather!

New England Clam Chowder
Kathy Van Daalen
Virginia Beach, VA

I have been making this recipe for years...I call it my almost-homemade clam chowder! It's delicious, easy to make and wonderful on a cold winter's day. Serve with hot buttered rolls.

4 slices bacon
1/2 c. onion, diced
4 stalks celery, diced
2 15-oz. cans New England
   clam chowder
6-1/2 oz. can baby clams,
   partially drained

2 c. milk
2 c. half-and-half
2 T. butter
1/2 t. salt
1/2 t. pepper
Garnish: chopped fresh parsley

In a skillet over medium heat, cook bacon until crisp. Remove bacon to a paper towel; reserve drippings in skillet. Sauté onion and celery in reserved drippings for about 5 minutes. Transfer onion mixture to a large saucepan; add crumbled bacon and remaining ingredients except garnish. Heat through over medium heat; do not boil. Serve hot, garnished with parsley. Makes 6 servings.

If there's a historic village nearby, bundle up the kids and go for a visit. Many times there will be special holiday programs...strolling carolers in period costumes, sleigh rides or special recitals in the town hall. Back home, warm up with a big pot of hot soup. Memories in the making!

Wonderful Winter Chowder

Debbie Hammer
New Hyde Park, NY

This is my Grandma Helen's recipe, loved by all.

1/2 c. butter, sliced	1 lb. scrod or cod, cubed
1 onion, chopped	15-oz. can corn, drained
2 potatoes, peeled and cubed	12-oz. can evaporated milk
2 c. water	salt and pepper to taste

Melt butter in a large saucepan over medium heat. Add onion; sauté until soft. Add potatoes and water; cook until potatoes are tender, about 15 to 20 minutes. Do not drain. Add fish and cook for a few minutes, until it flakes easily. Add corn and evaporated milk; heat through. Season with salt and pepper. Makes 8 servings.

Easy Potato Soup

Gladys Brehm
Quakertown, PA

I came up with this simple slow-cooker recipe years ago, when money was tight and I had to work long hours. It's a keeper!

6 potatoes, peeled and diced	2 c. whipping cream
1 to 2 onions, peeled and diced	salt and pepper to taste
12-oz. can evaporated milk	

To a 5-quart slow cooker, add potatoes, onion and just enough water to cover ingredients. Cover and cook on high setting for 2 to 3 hours, until potatoes are tender. Add evaporated milk and cream. Turn setting to low; cook until heated through, about one hour. Season with salt and pepper. Makes 6 to 8 servings.

Crunchy bread sticks are tasty soup dippers.
Stand them up in a colorful snack pail...
they'll take up little space on a soup buffet.

Slow-Cooker Tortilla Soup

Lori Sporer
Oakley, KS

This recipe was shared by a college friend. She raved about it prior to serving it to me...and it has been a favorite ever since! I have made this at the request of my 4-Hers for our group ski trip several years in a row! This soup freezes like a dream too. I often make it and freeze in individual containers to enjoy on short notice.

15-oz. can diced tomatoes
   with green chiles
15-oz. can corn
15-oz. can black beans
15-oz. can chili beans
15-oz. can navy beans

14-oz. can chicken broth
10-3/4 oz. can tomato soup
2 c. cooked chicken breast, diced
Garnish: crushed tortilla chips,
   shredded Cheddar cheese,
   sour cream

In a 5-quart slow cooker, combine tomatoes, corn and beans; do not drain vegetables. Add broth, soup and chicken. Cover and cook on low setting for 8 hours, or all day. Soup may also be made on the stovetop. Combine all ingredients except garnish in a stockpot and heat over medium heat for 30 to 45 minutes, stirring occasionally, until heated through. Ladle soup into bowls. Top with tortilla chips, cheese and a generous dollop of sour cream. Serves 8.

Save room in the freezer! Ladle extra soup into plastic zipping bags, seal and press flat. Lay the bags flat on a baking sheet and freeze. The frozen bags will stack easily.

Lynn Da's Chili

Linda Nunan
Baltimore, MD

*I have made this recipe ever since my children were very young...
that was over 30 years ago! It holds many dear memories of us all
sitting around the table enjoying good food and lots of love together.
Delicious served with Italian bread & butter.*

2 lbs. ground beef
1/2 c. onion, grated
1/2 c. green pepper, grated
1/2 c. red pepper, grated
3 15-1/2 oz. cans red
   kidney beans
15-1/2 oz. can diced tomatoes
10-3/4 oz. can tomato soup

2 T. baking cocoa
1 t. chili powder
1 t. onion powder
1/8 t. salt
1/8 t. pepper
2 c. cooked small elbow
   macaroni

In a soup pot over medium heat, brown beef with onion and peppers.
Drain; add remaining ingredients except macaroni. Add enough water
to fill soup pot half-full. Bring to a boil; reduce heat to low. Cover and
simmer for about 45 minutes, stirring occasionally. Stir in cooked
macaroni just before serving. Makes 8 servings.

There's no such thing as too much chili! Freeze leftovers in small
containers, to be microwaved and spooned over hot dogs or baked
potatoes. You can even spoon chili into flour tortillas and sprinkle
with shredded cheese for quick burritos. A busy-day life-saver!

Nora's Apple Bread

Wendy Perry
Midland, VA

This was my Grandma Nora's recipe. We looked forward to the delicious smells wafting through the air when the weather cooled.

8-oz. container sour cream
3/4 c. sugar
1/4 c. brown sugar, packed
2 eggs, beaten
1 T. vanilla extract
2 c. all-purpose flour
2 t. baking powder

1/2 t. baking soda
1 T. apple pie spice
1/2 t. salt
2 c. Granny Smith apple, peeled,
   cored and chopped
1 c. chopped pecans

Combine sour cream, sugars, eggs and vanilla in a large bowl. Beat with an electric mixer on low speed until blended; set aside. In a separate bowl, mix flour, baking powder, baking soda, spice and salt. Add flour mixture to sour cream mixture; beat on low speed until blended. With a spoon, stir in apples and pecans. Pour batter into a greased 9"x5" loaf pan. Bake at 350 degrees for one hour, or until a toothpick comes out clean. Makes one loaf.

A loaf of homemade fruit bread is always a welcome gift!
Make sure it stays fresh and tasty...let the bread cool completely
before wrapping well in plastic wrap or aluminum foil.

Quick & Easy Walnut Bread

Mel Chencharick
Julian, PA

I love all kinds of bread! The nice thing about this recipe is only five ingredients, no yeast and no waiting for dough to rise. Simple, simple, simple. I like hazelnuts, so sometimes I'll substitute them for the walnuts.

1/2 c. sugar
1 egg, beaten
1-1/4 c. milk

1-1/4 c. chopped walnuts
3 c. biscuit baking mix

In a large bowl, mix sugar, egg and milk; fold in walnuts. Stir in biscuit mix; beat very well for about 30 seconds to a minute. Pour batter into a well greased 9"x5" loaf pan. Bake at 350 degrees for 45 minutes. Makes one loaf.

My great-grandparents immigrated from Ireland with many kids to land out in the middle of Minnesota in a little town called Waverly, Minnesota. The early records of our church show that my family were some of our original charter members. The church they founded can be seen for many miles because of its unique pillar spires. Recently St. Mary's was ranked as one of the top ten most beautiful churches in Minnesota. On Christmas Eve, I bring our now-fifth generation of O'Connell grandkids to mass. I always tell my children it was because of a couple of very poor Irish immigrants deciding to come to America that they are blessed with the life they have now. What amazes me is that so many of our congregation still do the same thing I do.
At Christmas, my extended Waverly family all comes home.
That's what Christmas is about!

–Amy O'Connell, Eagan, MN

Portuguese Red Beans & Potatoes

Kelly Medeiros Morris
Marion, VA

This recipe from my Grandmother Viola Medeiros has been in our family for as long as I can remember. We usually add chouriço (Portuguese sausage) when we can get it here in Virginia. Serve with French bread.

5 to 6 potatoes, peeled and diced
1 T. bacon drippings or olive oil
1/2 c. onion, finely chopped
2 cloves garlic, minced
Optional: 1/4 lb. chourico
   sausage link, casing removed
   and cubed

2 16-oz. cans light red kidney
   beans, drained
15-oz. can tomato sauce
2 c. water
salt and pepper to taste

In a soup pot, cover potatoes with water. Bring to a boil over medium-high heat; simmer until partially tender. Meanwhile, add drippings or oil to a skillet over medium heat. Sauté onion, garlic and chourico, if using. Drain potatoes and return to pot. Add onion mixture, kidney beans, tomato sauce, water, salt and pepper. Cook over medium heat until all ingredients are fully cooked. Makes 6 to 8 servings.

Soup is extra hearty served in bread bowls. Cut the tops
off round crusty loaves and scoop out the soft bread inside.
Brush with olive oil. Bake at 350 degrees for a few
minutes until toasty, then ladle in hot soup.

Snowy Day
Soups & Breads

White Chicken Chili

Joyceann Dreibelbis
Wooster, OH

*So easy! You can have this healthy chili in the slow cooker
in just a few minutes and let it do all the work.*

4 cooked chicken breasts,
   shredded
48-oz. jar Great Northern
   beans, drained
2 c. chicken broth
1 c. salsa

1 T. dried cumin
salt and pepper to taste
2 c. shredded Cheddar cheese
Garnish: shredded Cheddar
   cheese, sour cream,
   saltine crackers

Add all ingredients except cheese and garnish to a 4 to 5-quart slow
cooker; stir. Cover and cook on high setting for 5 to 6 hours, or on
low setting for 10 to 12 hours. Add cheese in the last one to 2 hours;
cover and continue cooking. Garnish as desired. Serves 6 to 8.

Teresa's Best Skillet Cornbread

Teresa Eller
Kansas City, KS

*This recipe is picture-perfect. One of my friends told me
it should be in a magazine! Serve with creamery-fresh butter.*

1/4 c. canola oil
1 c. yellow cornmeal
1 c. all-purpose flour
1/4 c. sugar

1 T. baking powder
1 t. salt
1 egg, beaten
1 c. milk

Place oil in a 10" cast-iron skillet. Turn to coat; set in a 350-degree
oven. Meanwhile, in a bowl, combine cornmeal, flour, sugar, baking
powder and salt. Add egg and milk; mix well. Pour warm oil from
skillet into batter; stir. Pour batter into skillet. Turn oven to
400 degrees. Bake for 20 to 25 minutes. Remove from oven;
let cornbread set in the skillet for about 5 minutes. Turn out onto
a plate; cut into wedges. Makes 6 to 8 servings.

Greek Lemon Chicken Soup

Jo Ann Kurtz
Wichita Falls, TX

There used to be a Greek restaurant near us that served the best lemon chicken soup. When the owners retired, I figured out how to make it myself. Now I make it for our church soup suppers and I'm always asked for the recipe. Serve with warm bread.

8 c. chicken broth
1/2 c. long-cooking rice, uncooked
1/2 c. carrot, peeled and finely diced
1/2 c. celery, finely diced
2 c. cold milk
6 T. cornstarch

6 egg yolks, beaten
2 c. cooked chicken breast, chopped
1/4 c. butter, sliced
3/4 c. lemon juice
zest of 1 lemon
1/4 c. fresh parsley, chopped
salt and pepper to taste

In a saucepan over medium-high heat, bring broth to a boil. Stir in uncooked rice, carrot and celery. Cover and cook until rice is tender, about 25 minutes. Meanwhile, in a bowl, stir together milk and cornstarch; beat in egg yolks and set aside. Remove saucepan from heat. Slowly add milk and egg mixture, stirring as you add it. Continue stirring until soup thickens. Add remaining ingredients; stir well. Makes 8 to 10 servings.

When purchasing a fresh-cut Christmas tree, ask about trimmed-off branches. They're often available at little or no cost and are so handy for adding seasonal color and fresh pine scent to your home.

Roasted Cauliflower Soup

Lori Rosenberg
University Heights, OH

For a cold winter day after a snow shoveling party or building awesome snow people, this soup really takes off the chills!

1 head cauliflower, cut into
    flowerets
3 T. oil, divided
salt and pepper to taste
1 onion, diced
2 cloves garlic, chopped

1 t. fresh rosemary, finely
    chopped
3 c. vegetable or chicken broth
1-1/2 c. shredded white Cheddar
    cheese
1 c. light cream or milk

On a large baking sheet, toss cauliflower flowerets with 2 tablespoons oil, salt and pepper. Arrange in a single layer. Bake, uncovered, at 400 degrees for 20 to 30 minutes, until lightly golden. Meanwhile, heat remaining oil in a large saucepan over medium heat. Add onion and sauté until tender, 5 to 7 minutes. Add garlic and rosemary; sauté until fragrant, about one minute. Add broth and bring to a boil, scraping up any dark bits from the bottom of the pan. Add cauliflower; return to a boil. Reduce heat to low; cover and simmer for 20 minutes. Purée soup to desired consistency with an immersion blender. Stir in cheese and allow to melt; do not boil. Remove from heat. Stir in cream or milk; season with salt and pepper. Makes 4 servings.

Dress up bowls of soup for the season in a jiffy. Use a mini cookie cutter to cut stars from a slice of cheese.

6-Bean Country Soup

Sarah Slaven
Strunk, KY

This is my family's favorite dish. It gets better each time!

1/2 c. dried red beans
1/2 c. dried navy beans
1/2 c. dried pinto beans
1/2 c. baby lima beans
1/2 c. dried kidney beans
1/2 c. dried Great Northern
    beans
28-oz. can diced tomatoes
4 to 5 c. water
2 cubes beef bouillon
2 T. dried minced onion

1 T. dried parsley
1 t. Italian seasoning
1 t. dried minced garlic
1 t. dried thyme
1/2 t. dried oregano
1/2 t. pepper
1/4 t. red pepper flakes
2 bay leaves
1 lb. smoked pork sausage link,
    sliced, or 2 smoked ham
    hocks

Combine beans in a large bowl. Cover with water; let soak for 6 hours to overnight. Drain beans, discarding water. In a Dutch oven, combine beans, tomatoes with juice, 4 to 5 cups water and remaining ingredients. Stir well; bring to a boil over high heat. Reduce heat to low; cover and simmer for 1-1/2 to 2 hours, stirring occasionally, until beans are tender. Before serving, discard bay leaves. If using ham hocks, remove from soup and cut off the ham, returning it to the soup. Makes 8 to 10 servings.

A favorite cook would love receiving a gift of a soup "kit."
Fill a red-speckled enamelware soup pot with soup bowls,
oversized table napkins and a soup ladle. Tuck in a favorite
recipe and a package or two of dried beans.

Pops' Corned Beef Vegetable Soup

Jessica Musetti
Columbus, OH

Every year as the weather turned cooler, my Papa Coleman used to make this soup for us. Instead of the traditional beef everyone else used, Pops used corned beef. It was a nod to our Scottish ancestry and remains my favorite soup to this day.

12-oz. can corned beef, flaked
28-oz. can whole tomatoes, mashed
16-oz. can green beans, drained
15-oz. can corn, drained
15-1/4 oz. can peas, drained
1/2 head cabbage, coarsely chopped

4 to 5 russet potatoes, peeled and diced
1/2 lb. baby carrots
1 yellow onion, diced
1/2 c. catsup, or to taste
1 t. red pepper flakes
salt and pepper to taste
hot pepper sauce to taste

In a large soup pot, combine corned beef, tomatoes with juice and remaining ingredients. Add enough water to fill pot halfway. Bring to a boil over high heat; return heat to medium. Simmer for 30 to 40 minutes, stirring occasionally, until potatoes and carrots are tender. Reduce heat to low; simmer for another 20 minutes. Serves 6 to 8.

Snowy paper-white narcissus flowers are a winter delight that Grandmother loved. Place paper-white bulbs in water-filled bulb vases, pointed ends up. Set in a sunny window. In about 6 weeks you'll have blooms!

Cranberry Yeast Rolls

Gerri Roth
Flushing, MI

*I created this recipe to use at Christmas time. I love cinnamon rolls
and was looking to make something a little different.*

2 envs. active dry yeast
1/4 c. very warm water, 110 to
   115 degrees
1 c. very warm milk, 110 to
   115 degrees
1/2 c. butter, sliced
1/4 c. sugar

1 t. salt
4 c. all-purpose flour, divided
2 eggs, beaten
15-oz. can whole-berry
   cranberry sauce
1 t. cinnamon, divided

In a cup, dissolve yeast in warm water; set aside. In a large bowl, pour
warm milk over butter, sugar and salt. Let stand for 5 to 10 minutes.
Add yeast mixture to milk mixture. Stir in 2 cups flour; beat in eggs.
Add remaining flour and mix well. Cover and refrigerate dough for
2 hours to overnight. Divide dough in half. Roll out half of dough on
a floured surface to 1/4-inch thick. Spread half of cranberry sauce over
dough, to 1/4-inch from edge of dough. Sprinkle with 1/2 teaspoon
cinnamon. Roll up dough, starting on one long edge; slice into
12 spirals. Place rolls cut-side down in a greased 13"x9" baking pan.
Repeat with remaining dough, sauce, cinnamon and another pan.
Cover pans; let rise for 30 minutes. Bake at 350 degrees for 25 to
30 minutes, until golden. Makes 2 dozen.

Tie ornaments onto the Christmas
tree with narrow strips of homespun
fabric...sweet and simple! Handy if
little ones or pets are in the
household, too.

Cozy Meals
for Busy Days

Michelle's Yum Chicken

Rebecca Etling
Blairsville, PA

This is my youngest daughter's very favorite recipe.

4 boneless, skinless chicken
    breasts
2 T. seasoning salt
6 slices bacon

2 T. olive oil
Optional: 1 c. sliced mushrooms
2 c. shredded Cheddar cheese

Pound chicken breasts to 1/2-inch thickness; rub with seasoning salt. Cover and refrigerate for one hour. Meanwhile, arrange bacon slices on a paper towel-lined microwave-safe plate. Cover with another paper towel; microwave for 6 minutes, or until crisp. Set aside. In a skillet over medium heat, sauté chicken in oil for 3 to 5 minutes per side, until golden. Arrange chicken in a lightly greased 13"x9" baking pan. Spread Honey Mustard Sauce over chicken; layer with mushrooms, if using, crumbled bacon and cheese. Bake, uncovered, at 350 degrees for 30 minutes, or until chicken juices run clear when pierced and cheese is melted. Serve with remaining sauce. Makes 4 servings.

Honey Mustard Sauce:

1/4 c. mustard
1/3 c. honey

3 T. mayonnaise
2 t. dried minced onion

Combine all ingredients; mix well.

Turn Christmas cards into festive napkin rings. Cut them into strips with decorative-edge scissors, join ends with craft glue and add a sprig of faux holly...simple!

Mom's Pasta, Chicken, Trees & Cheese

Mary Therese Onoshko
Point Pleasant, NJ

My four teenagers love this recipe! It's simple and quick to make on busy evenings between games and practice. Sometimes I prepare the recipe ahead and bring it to the field or gym as an alternative to a fast-food dinner. To save time, all the ingredients can cook at the same time. You can even use pre-cooked chicken if pressed for time.

16-oz. pkg. rigatoni pasta, uncooked
1 lb. boneless chicken breasts, cut into strips or large cubes
salt, pepper and favorite onion & garlic seasoning to taste

3 T. oil
2 c. broccoli flowerets
1 T. butter
2 c. Parmesan cheese, shaved

Cook pasta according to package directions; drain. Meanwhile, season chicken strips as desired. Heat oil in a skillet over medium heat; add chicken. Cook for 4 to 5 minutes, until chicken juices run clear when pierced; drain and set aside. In a saucepan over high heat, bring one inch water to a boil. Add broccoli and cook for 5 to 6 minutes, until tender; drain. Return cooked pasta to pot; immediately add butter, cheese, chicken and broccoli. Stir gently until all ingredients are well combined. Cover and keep warm to allow cheese to melt a little more. Serves 6.

A cheery welcome at the front door! Tie a bundle of evergreen clippings to a rustic twig broom with a jaunty red bow.

Dad's Goulash

Laura Flores
Middletown, CT

My dad made up this recipe to try and recreate a dish that his mother used to make for him back in the 1930s. It's fast, easy, economical and nutritious...the kids will love it too.

1 lb. ground beef
2 28-oz. cans crushed tomatoes
15-oz. can tomato sauce
1 t. onion powder

1 t. salt
2 c. elbow macaroni, uncooked
Optional: grated Romano or
    Parmesan cheese

Brown beef in a deep skillet over medium heat; drain. Add tomatoes with juice, tomato sauce and seasonings to beef. Reduce heat to low; cover and simmer for 15 minutes. Meanwhile, cook macaroni according to package directions; drain. Stir cooked macaroni into beef mixture; heat through. Serve topped with cheese, if desired. Makes 6 servings.

A veggie-packed topiary will certainly "spruce" up your buffet table! Cover a 12-inch styrofoam cone with aluminum foil. Attach broccoli flowerets and cherry tomatoes by sticking one end of a toothpick into the veggie and the other end into the cone. Garnish with cheese "ornaments."

Grandma Baker's Macaroni

Kathy Rixham
Reisterstown, MD

This recipe is versatile as well as delicious! It makes two casseroles and can be served as either a main or a side dish. Italian bread & butter goes very well with it.

16-oz. pkg. large elbow
   macaroni, uncooked
3/4 c. butter, divided
2 to 3 onions, sliced
3/4 lb. sharp Cheddar cheese,
   diced

4 to 5 6-oz. cans tomato paste
1/2 c. dry bread crumbs, or to
   taste
1/2 c. grated Parmesan cheese,
   or to taste

Cook pasta according to package directions; drain. Meanwhile, melt 1/4 cup butter in a skillet over medium heat. Sauté onions until tender. Add onion mixture and cheese to cooked macaroni; mix well. Add tomato paste, rinsing each can with a little water and adding this to macaroni as well. Divide mixture between 2 greased 2-1/2 quart casserole dishes. Sprinkle each with bread crumbs and Parmesan cheese. Thinly slice remaining butter; dot each casserole with 5 pats, one in each corner and one in the center. Bake, uncovered, at 350 degrees for about 45 minutes, until bubbly and top is lightly golden. Casseroles may be covered and frozen before baking; thaw completely in the refrigerator and bake as above. Makes 2 casseroles; each serves 4.

Warm garlic bread makes any meal a little better! Blend together 1/2 cup softened butter with 2 minced garlic cloves, one tablespoon chopped parsley and 1/4 cup grated Parmesan cheese. Split a loaf of Italian bread and spread both halves with the butter. Broil for 2 to 3 minutes, until golden and bubbly. Slice and serve.

Pepper Steak

Brenda Hager
Nancy, KY

*I have made this comfort food for many, many years...now my
daughter Stephanie makes it for her own family.*

2 T. oil
1-1/2 lbs. beef round steak,
   cut into 1-inch wide strips
1 onion, chopped
1 c. beef broth
3 T. less-sodium soy sauce
1 clove garlic, minced

2 green peppers, cut into 1-inch
   wide strips
1/4 c. cold water
2 T. cornstarch
2 tomatoes, cut into thin wedges
4 c. cooked rice

Heat oil in a large skillet or Dutch oven over medium heat; add beef
strips and cook until browned. Add onion and cook until tender; drain.
Stir in broth, soy sauce and garlic. Reduce heat to medium-low; cover
and simmer for 10 minutes. Add green peppers; simmer an additional
5 minutes. In a cup, blend water and cornstarch to make a smooth
paste. Add slowly to skillet, stirring constantly until mixture thickens
and boils. Boil and stir for one minute. Add tomatoes; heat through.
Serve over cooked rice. Makes 4 to 6 servings.

The whole family would get together at my grandma's on Christmas
Eve. There was just so much excitement in the air! We would share
a nice dinner, then Grandma would have all of the cousins sit down
in the living room and she would tell us Christmas stories. Then there
would be a lot of noise on the porch and a knock on the door. One of
my aunts would open the door and announce, "Look who's here to
see you children. It's Santa!" Santa would stop and talk to each one
of us children and he handed out gifts to everyone. On the way out
the door, Santa made us all promise to go to bed as soon as we
got home, so that he could visit us sometime during the night.
We felt the excitement all the way home!

–Karla Himpelmann, Morris, IL

Stir-Fry Pork & Noodles

*Linda Cuellar
Riverside, CA*

This is a quick and tasty meal, very easy to prepare. It's one of my go-to meals. I like to serve an Asian salad with this dish.

12-oz. pkg. thin egg noodles,
   uncooked
1/2 lb. boneless pork, cubed
1 T. oil
2 lbs. fresh bean sprouts, rinsed
   and drained

4 to 5 green onions, chopped
   and divided
2 eggs, beaten
3 T. light soy sauce
salt and pepper to taste

Cook noodles according to package directions; drain. Meanwhile, in a skillet over medium-high heat, brown pork cubes in oil; drain. Stir in bean sprouts and half of green onions; heat through. Stir eggs into pork mixture; cook until almost done. Stir in soy sauce, salt and pepper. Add cooked noodles; mix well. Sprinkle with remaining onions and serve. Makes 4 servings.

Stir-frying is a terrific way to make a delicious busy-day dinner.
Slice meats and veggies into equal-size pieces before you start
cooking...they'll all be done to perfection at the same time.

Christmas Comfort Classics

Crispy Baked Chicken Tenders
Tracy Meyers
Alexandria, KY

Who doesn't love chicken tenders? My daughter Madison asks for these over anything else, fast food or frozen! I came up with this recipe when the hushpuppy mix and potato flakes were all I had in the pantry. Who knew it would be such a hit!

3 to 4 boneless, skinless chicken
    breasts
2 eggs, beaten
1/4 c. milk
1/2 c. instant mashed potato
    flakes

1/3 c. hushpuppy mix
1 T. seasoned salt
salt and pepper to taste
2 to 3 T. butter, thinly sliced

Cut each chicken breast lengthwise into 3 to 4 tenders; set aside. In a small dish, whisk together eggs and milk. In a separate dish, combine potato flakes, hushpuppy mix and seasoned salt. Dip each chicken tender into egg mixture, then into potato flake mixture. Arrange tenders on a baking sheet sprayed with non-stick vegetable spray. Season with a little salt and pepper; place 2 to 3 thin pats of butter on each tender so the coating will become crisp. Bake at 350 degrees for 20 to 25 minutes, until crisp, golden and chicken juices run clear when pierced. Serves 4.

The perfect Christmas tree? All Christmas trees are perfect!

–Charles N. Barnard

Sausage Pockets

Lorretta Johnson
Wolcottville, IN

I wanted a quick delicious meal and came up with this yummy recipe. My family loves it and so do I!

1 lb. ground pork sausage
1/2 c. onion, chopped
1/4 t. garlic, minced
salt and pepper to taste
Optional: 1 T. fresh cilantro,
   chopped

8-oz. tube refrigerated crescent
   rolls
3 T. shredded Cheddar cheese
1/4 t. garlic powder
Optional: grated Parmesan
   cheese

Brown sausage, onion and garlic in a skillet over medium heat; drain. Add salt, pepper and cilantro, if using; mix well and remove from heat. Unroll crescent rolls; separate into 8 triangles. Divide sausage mixture among the triangles; top each with one teaspoon cheese. Fold over each triangle; seal edges with your fingers or a fork. Place on an ungreased baking sheet. Sprinkle with garlic powder and Parmesan cheese, if desired. Bake at 375 degrees for 12 to 15 minutes, until golden. Makes 8 servings.

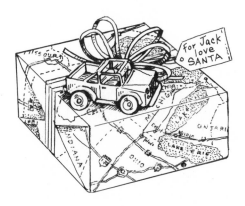

Clever gift wrap...try the newspaper comic pages, road maps, pretty fabric or copies of the kids' artwork. They'll love it!

Quick One-Pot Burrito Bowl

Sarah Lundvall
Ephrata, PA

This is one of those go-to meals I fix on nights when we get home late from work and want dinner quickly.

3 T. olive oil
1/2 c. onion, chopped
1 clove garlic, minced
1 cooked chicken breast, diced
1 c. long-cooking brown rice,
    uncooked
14-oz. can chicken broth
14-1/2 oz. can diced tomatoes
    with green chiles

15-1/2 oz. can light red kidney
    beans, drained and rinsed
11-oz. can corn, drained
1 T. dried cumin
2 t. chili powder
1/2 t. garlic powder
1/4 t. pepper
2 c. shredded Cheddar cheese

Heat oil in a skillet over medium heat. Sauté onion and garlic until translucent. Add chicken and cook for 2 minutes. Add uncooked rice; cook and stir until lightly toasted. Stir in broth, tomatoes with juice and remaining ingredients except cheese. Bring to a boil; reduce heat to low. Cover and simmer for 25 minutes, or until liquid is mostly absorbed. Turn off heat. Uncover and sprinkle with cheese. Cover and let stand for 3 to 5 minutes, until cheese is melted. Makes 4 servings.

Share the cheer! Invite party guests to bring along a can of food. Gather all the cans in a big wicker basket and drop it off at a local food pantry.

Cozy Meals
for Busy Days

Su-Lin's Tex-Mex Rolls

Rudie Shahinian
Ontario, Canada

My daughter Coco had a dear Korean friend, Su-Lin, who came up with this recipe while we were having Mexican Night at our house. These Asian-Mexican fusion rolls were a huge hit...we've been making them ever since.

1 lb. ground beef
1-oz. pkg. taco seasoning mix
2 T. hot pepper sauce
15-oz. can whole baby sweet
  corn
8-oz. can sliced water chestnuts,
  drained

2 c. peas, thawed if frozen
2 to 3 8-oz. tubes refrigerated
  crescent rolls
2 c. shredded Cheddar cheese
Garnish: sour cream, salsa,
  chopped green onions

Brown beef in a skillet over medium heat; drain. Stir in taco seasoning, hot sauce, baby corn with juice, water chestnuts and peas; heat through. Unroll crescent rolls; separate into triangles. Place 3 tablespoons beef mixture on each triangle; sprinkle with cheese and roll up. Place on an ungreased baking sheet. Bake at 375 degrees for 15 to 20 minutes, until golden. Serve with sour cream, chopped green onion and salsa. Makes 8 servings.

With houses decorated for the holidays, it's a great time to host a progressive dinner with family & friends. Enjoy appetizers at one home, then visit other homes for the salad, main course and dessert.

Potato Cake

Eleanor Dionne
Beverly, MA

This is one of my mom's recipes that I have made through the years. It's a great potato side dish that's a little different.

4 baking potatoes
2 T. butter
1 Spanish onion, finely chopped
salt and pepper to taste
1/8 t. allspice

4 eggs, lightly beaten
1/3 c. all-purpose flour
1 T. fresh rosemary, chopped
3 T. canola oil

Peel potatoes; set aside in a bowl of cold water. Melt butter in a skillet over medium heat. Add onion; sprinkle with salt, pepper and allspice. Cook for about 10 minutes; remove from heat. Drain potatoes and pat dry. With a food processor or cheese grater, shred potatoes. Add onion mixture to potatoes along with eggs, flour and rosemary; mix well. Brush a 10" round baking pan with oil, coating bottom and sides of pan well. Heat oiled pan in the oven at 350 degrees for 2 minutes. Carefully remove pan; pour potato mixture into pan. Smooth the top and return to oven. Bake at 350 degrees for 35 to 45 minutes, until set and golden. Remove from oven; let stand for a few minutes before cutting into wedges. Serves 4.

Bring a bit of retro to the holiday kitchen...
tie on a vintage Christmas apron!

Crumb-Topped Vegetable Medley   *Vickie*

Delicious and so easy! Try it with other veggie blends too.

16-oz. pkg. frozen broccoli,
　　cauliflower & carrot blend
salt and pepper to taste
1 T. butter
1 T. olive oil

1/2 c. dry bread crumbs
1 clove garlic, minced
1 t. lemon zest
1 T. fresh parsley, chopped

Cook frozen vegetables according to package directions. Drain and transfer to a serving bowl. Season with salt and pepper; cover and set aside. Melt butter with oil in a saucepan over medium-high heat. Add bread crumbs and garlic; cook and stir until golden. Remove from heat; stir in lemon zest and parsley. Top vegetables with crumb mixture; serve. Makes 4 to 6 servings.

Green Beans & Zucchini   *Linda Shively*
Hopkinsville, KY

This is one of our favorites year 'round. A great use of zucchini!

4 slices bacon
1/4 c. butter
1/2 c. onion, chopped
2 to 3 zucchini, thinly sliced

15-oz. can French-cut green
　　beans, drained
3/4 t. salt
1/8 t. pepper

In a large skillet, cook bacon until crisp; remove bacon to a paper towel. Pour drippings from skillet and discard; wipe skillet with a paper towel. Add butter and onion; cook until onion is soft. Add zucchini and stir-fry until done. Stir in green beans, crumbled bacon, salt and pepper; heat through. Makes 6 to 8 servings.

Hide a small wrapped gift in the Christmas tree for each member of the family to find when putting away the ornaments.

Chicken Stroganoff

Leona Krivda
Belle Vernon, PA

Everyone at my house looks forward to this dinner. With a buttered vegetable on the side and some crusty bread, it is a nice supper.

6 boneless, skinless chicken
   breasts
garlic powder, salt and pepper
   to taste
10-3/4 oz. can cream of
   mushroom soup

8-oz. pkg. cream cheese,
   softened and cubed
12-oz. pkg. wide egg noodles,
   uncooked
16-oz. container sour cream,
   divided

Spray a 5-quart slow cooker with non-stick vegetable spray. Season chicken breasts as desired; arrange in slow cooker. Top with soup and cream cheese. Cover and cook on low setting for 6 to 8 hours, stirring twice, until chicken is very tender. About 20 minutes before serving time, cook noodles according to package directions; drain well. Shred chicken with 2 forks; stir back into mixture in slow cooker. Add 3/4 of the sour cream; mix well. Add cooked noodles to chicken mixture; stir gently. Just before serving, stir in remaining sour cream. Makes 6 servings.

A festive touch for your holiday table...a wreath of rolls! Looks pretty on a cake stand too. Arrange unbaked dinner rolls in a ring on a parchment paper-lined baking sheet. Brush with butter, sprinkle with green herbs and bake as directed.

Grandma's Pot Roast

Brenda Graham
Clarendon Hills, IL

My grandma always made the best pot roast. She made hers in the oven, as does my mom. My sister has the best luck making pot roast on the stovetop, and I enjoy it most from my slow cooker. It is so easy, so tender and yummy! I like to serve this with mashed potatoes and green beans. Ever since I was a little girl I have always loved having the leftover roast on bread with a little bit of catsup!

3 to 4-lb. beef chuck roast
1 to 2 T. oil
1 c. water
1 t. salt
6 to 8 whole cloves
3 bay leaves

Heat oil in a skillet over medium-high heat. Add roast and brown on all sides. Combine water and salt in a 5 to 6-quart slow cooker. Add roast to slow cooker. Stud roast with cloves; arrange bay leaves on top. Cover and cook on low setting for 8 hours, or until very tender. Discard bay leaves and cloves before serving. Makes 4 to 6 servings.

Homemade pan gravy is simple to make. Remove the roast to a platter and pour the pan juices into a large saucepan over medium heat. Shake together 1/4 cup cold water and 1/4 cup cornstarch in a small jar; add to the pan. Cook and stir until gravy comes to a boil and thickens, 5 to 10 minutes. Season with salt and pepper, and it's ready to serve.

Christmas Comfort Classics

Easy Pulled Pork for a Crowd

Pauletta Dove
Williamson, WV

A great way to make a lot of people happy! My work crew loves this and asks for it often. You can add chili powder, hot sauce, whatever you like to suit your taste.

18-oz. bottle favorite barbecue
    sauce, divided
5 lbs. country-style pork ribs,
    cut into serving-size portions

1/2 c. water
salt and pepper to taste
2 onions, sliced

Spread 1/2 cup barbecue sauce in the bottom of a 6-quart slow cooker. Layer ribs over sauce; top with remaining sauce. Add water, salt and pepper; layer onion slices on top. Cover and cook on high setting for 3 hours. Turn setting to low and continue cooking for 5 to 6 hours. May also be cooked only on low setting for 10 to 12 hours. Remove ribs to a platter. Pull apart with 2 forks, discarding bones and any large pieces of fat. Ladle some of the sauce and onions from slow cooker over pork. Makes 20 to 25 servings.

Whether it's a game-day gathering or a post-caroling supper, holiday get-togethers don't need to be formal. Pulled-meat sandwiches are perfect. Just add lots of warm buns, a big tossed salad, cookies for dessert and plenty of paper napkins!

Celery Seed Slaw

*Sandra Sullivan
Aurora, CO*

*A simple cooked dressing gives crisp cabbage a delightful
break from mayonnaise-based coleslaw. It's perfect for potlucks.*

3 lbs. cabbage, chopped
1/2 c. carrot, peeled and
   shredded
1/2 c. green pepper, chopped

1 c. cider vinegar
1 c. sugar
1 T. salt
1 t. celery seed

Combine cabbage, carrot and green pepper in a heatproof bowl; set
aside. In a saucepan over medium heat, combine vinegar, sugar, salt
and celery seed. Bring to a boil; stir until sugar dissolves. Pour hot
vinegar mixture over cabbage mixture; toss well. Cover and refrigerate
for 4 hours to overnight. Toss again before serving. Makes 12 servings.

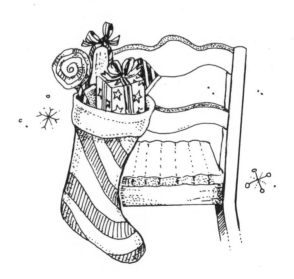

No fireplace? Hang stockings from stair railings,
doorknobs, bookshelves or the backs of chairs!

Cheesy Eggplant Casserole

Megan Brooks
Antioch, TN

My mom got this recipe from a neighborhood cookbook and made it often when I was growing up. Recently she gave me the recipe...I tried it and it's just as good as it used to be!

1 to 2 T. oil
1 eggplant, peeled and cut
    into strips or cubes
1 lb. ground beef
1/2 c. onion, chopped
15-oz. can tomato sauce
Italian seasoning and salt
    to taste

1/2 c. grated Parmesan cheese
8-oz. pkg. shredded mozzarella
    cheese
1/2 c. saltine crackers, crushed
1/4 c. butter, melted
Optional: additional grated
    Parmesan cheese

Heat oil in a skillet over medium heat. Sauté eggplant until tender; drain and set aside. Brown beef with onion in the same skillet; drain. Stir in tomato sauce and seasonings. Cook over low heat for several minutes, stirring occasionally. In a greased 9"x9" baking pan, layer half each of eggplant, beef mixture and Parmesan cheese. Repeat layers. Bake, uncovered, at 350 degrees for 25 minutes, or until eggplant is nearly tender. Top with mozzarella cheese; toss cracker crumbs with butter and sprinkle over cheese. Return to oven for an additional 5 to 10 minutes, until cheese is melted and crumb topping is golden. Serve with additional Parmesan cheese, if desired. Makes 4 servings.

Make time for your town's special holiday events. Whether it's a Christmas parade, Santa arriving by horse-drawn sleigh or a tree lighting ceremony, hometown traditions make the sweetest memories.

Chili Relleno Casserole

Charlene McCain
Bakersfield, CA

I first tasted this delicious cheesy dish at a potluck and begged for the recipe...since then, it's become one of my family's favorites. It's a quick and light meatless dish to make for supper that won't break the bank. My boys like it hot so I serve theirs with salsa. I like mine just the way it is. I serve this with an avocado & tomato salad.

1/2 c. butter, melted
2 7-oz. cans whole green chiles,
   drained
16-oz. pkg. shredded Cheddar
   Jack cheese
3 eggs, beaten

2 c. milk
3/4 t. salt
1 c. biscuit baking mix
Garnish: chopped green onions
Optional: salsa

Spread melted butter in a 13"x9" baking pan; set aside. Slice open chiles so insides are exposed. Arrange flattened chiles in a layer in bottom of pan; cover evenly with cheese. In a bowl, whisk together eggs, milk, salt and biscuit mix; pour over cheese. Bake, uncovered, at 350 degrees for 35 to 40 minutes, until golden. Sprinkle with green onions; serve with salsa, if desired. Makes 6 to 8 servings.

Have a homemade Christmas gift exchange? When names
are drawn, everyone agrees that all gifts are to be made by hand.
Remember to start early! You may be pleasantly surprised at
the clever ideas everyone comes up with.

Christmas Comfort Classics

Mom's Pork Chop & Rice Dinner
Joyce Borrill
Utica, NY

Mom also called this Meal in a Pan and it's a tasty one-dish dinner. It was one of her favorites. If you use a cast-iron skillet, you can pop it right into the oven.

4 pork chops, 1-inch thick
1 to 2 T. olive oil
1 c. long-cooking rice, uncooked
1 onion, chopped

1 green pepper, chopped
28-oz. can diced tomatoes
Optional: 1/2 c. shredded
    Cheddar cheese

In a cast-iron skillet over medium heat, brown chops in oil. Drain. If not using a cast-iron skillet, transfer chops to a greased 13"x9" baking pan. Sprinkle uncooked rice over chops; add onions, peppers and tomatoes with juice. Cover and bake at 375 degrees for one hour, or until rice is tender. If desired, uncover 5 minutes before done; top with cheese and bake another 5 minutes. Serves 4.

Onion-Baked Pork Chops
Shirley Howie
Foxboro, MA

This is a super-easy recipe that I turn to when I want a quick and tasty dinner. Any leftover chops are good reheated. I like to cut up the leftovers into small pieces, mix with mustard and mayo, and spoon into pita bread to make a pocket sandwich. Delish!

2 eggs
1.35-oz. pkg. onion soup mix

1/2 c. dry bread crumbs
8 pork chops, 1/2 inch thick

Beat eggs in a bowl; combine soup mix with bread crumbs in a separate bowl. Dip pork chops into eggs; coat well with bread crumb mixture. Arrange chops in a greased shallow 13"x9" baking pan. Bake, uncovered, at 400 degrees for 40 minutes, or until chops are tender and cooked through. Makes 8 servings.

Carrot Apple Slaw

Courtney Stultz
Weir, KS

*Coleslaw is so versatile and we use it with everything...
burgers, sandwiches, you name it! This has a nice flavor
and is great served with holiday meals.*

1 head purple cabbage, shredded
1 to 2 apples, cored and
   shredded
2 to 3 carrots, peeled and
   shredded
1 T. olive oil
2 T. water

2 t. cider vinegar
1 t. honey
1 t. garlic or onion powder
1 t. poppy seed
1 t. sea salt
1/2 t. pepper

In a large serving bowl, combine cabbage, apples and carrots; set aside. In a small bowl, whisk together remaining ingredients. Pour dressing over cabbage mixture and stir until combined. Cover and refrigerate about 30 minutes before serving. Makes 8 servings.

For a thoughtful gift that's sure to be appreciated, purchase a calendar and fill in birthdays, anniversaries, graduations and other important family events. Grandma will love it. It's a nice gift for anyone who's new to the family too.

Lucille's Sloppy Joes

Jacqueline Orszulak
La Porte, IN

My mother made these sandwiches to sell at her church's annual craft fair. Everyone loved them! She made them at home for showers and parties too. We always enjoyed them with potato chips.

3 lbs. ground beef
1-1/2 c. celery, chopped
1-1/2 c. onion, chopped
1 c. carrots, peeled and diced
7 T. brown sugar

1/4 c. vinegar
2 T. mustard seed
catsup to taste
20 hamburger buns, split

Brown beef in a large skillet over medium heat; drain. Stir in remaining ingredients except buns, adding enough catsup to moisten mixture. Bring to a boil; reduce heat to low. Simmer until vegetables are tender, stirring often. Serve beef mixture spooned onto hamburger buns. Makes 20 servings.

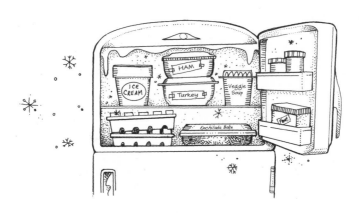

December is packed with things to do, so take it easy with simple, hearty meals. Make double batches of family favorites like chili and Sloppy Joes early in the holiday season and freeze half to heat & eat later. What a timesaver!

Mom's Hashbrown Casserole
Donna Cannon
Tulsa, OK

This casserole is a comfort food, filling and savory. Great for potluck dinners and get-togethers! My four active children just love this recipe and request it not just for dinner with hamburgers, but for birthday meals and even for breakfast. It is so easy that I have my grandchildren helping me. My grown son even asks to take a dish of this home. His wife knows how to fix it as well, but you know, Mom's food just always seems to taste better!

32-oz. pkg. frozen southern-style diced potatoes, thawed
2 to 3 c. shredded Colby Jack cheese, or more to taste
10-3/4 oz. can cream of chicken soup
1/2 c. onion, diced

16-oz. container regular or low-fat sour cream
1/2 to 1 t. salt
1/2 to 1 t. pepper
2 c. whole-grain rice or wheat flake cereal, crushed

Spray a 13"x9" baking pan with non-stick vegetable spray. Combine all ingredients except cereal in pan. Mix gently; spread out potato mixture evenly in pan. Sprinkle crushed cereal on top. Bake, uncovered, at 375 degrees for 50 to 60 minutes, until bubbly and cheese is melted. Remove from oven; let cool for several minutes before serving. Makes 10 to 12 servings.

Wind strands of glossy red wooden beads around a holiday buffet or evergreen wreath. They're as decorative as fresh cranberries, yet can be packed away to re-use next year.

Christmas Comfort Classics

Carol's Cheese Enchiladas

Carol Thompson
Casa Grande, AZ

This has become one of my children's favorite recipes. They requested it often when they were growing up. They never realized that I gradually tweaked it over the years to make it healthier!

8-oz. container low-fat sour
    cream
8-oz. pkg. low-fat cream cheese,
    softened
8-oz. pkg. low-fat shredded
    Cheddar cheese

1/2 c. onion, diced
4-oz. can chopped green chiles
10 8-inch flour tortillas
20-oz. can red or green
    enchilada sauce

In a large bowl, combine all ingredients except tortillas and enchilada sauce; mix well. Place 1/4 cup of mixture on the edge of each tortilla; roll up tightly. Spray a 13"x9" baking pan with non-stick vegetable spray. Place filled tortillas in pan, seam-side down. Spoon sauce over tortillas. Bake, covered, at 350 degrees for 25 to 30 minutes. Makes 10 servings.

Kris's Chicken Enchiladas

Kris Thompson
Ripley, NY

My kids are grown and I live alone, so I make this and freeze it in serving-size portions. Then, if someone drops in for lunch, it just needs to be thawed quickly in the microwave and heated through.

8-oz. pkg. cream cheese,
    softened
2 c. salsa, divided
2 c. cooked chicken breast,
    chopped

2 c. shredded Cheddar cheese,
    divided
10 8-inch flour tortillas

In a skillet over low heat, stir together cream cheese and one cup salsa until cream cheese is melted. Stir in chicken and one cup shredded cheese. Top each tortilla with 1/4 cup mixture; roll up. Spray a 13"x9" baking pan with non-stick vegetable spray. Place filled tortillas in pan, seam-side down. Top with remaining salsa. and cheese. Bake, uncovered, at 350 degrees for 25 to 30 minutes, until heated through and cheese is melted. Makes 10 servings.

Best Spanish Rice

*Alice Hardin
Antioch, CA*

*This is such an easy way to make Spanish rice and I have gotten
many requests for the recipe. That is the ultimate compliment!
I find cooking it in a electric skillet is the best way to make it.*

2 T. olive oil
2 T. onion, chopped
3 cloves garlic, minced
1-1/2 c. long-cooking rice,
    uncooked

2 c. chicken broth
1 c. mild or medium chunky
    salsa

Heat oil in an electric skillet or a stovetop skillet over medium heat.
Stir in onion and garlic; cook until tender, about 5 minutes. Add
uncooked rice to skillet. Cook and stir until rice begins to turn golden.
Stir in broth and salsa. Reduce heat and simmer for 20 minutes, or
until liquid is absorbed and rice is tender. Serves 4.

It was Christmas 1988 and our kids were six and three. The old dog
that we'd had before we had kids had passed away during Christmas
1987 and we all still missed her. On Christmas morning, we picked
up a golden retriever puppy, wrapped the outside of the box and
set it under the Christmas tree just before we woke the kids. The
puppy began barking and the kids found her pretty quickly. Her
name was Taffy and we had her for 16 years. You could not have
asked for a sweeter, more patient dog. She did not care what
the kids did, as long as they were paying attention to her.
She was a gift to all of us!

–Donna Riley, Browns Summit, NC

Black-Eyed Peas & Sausage

Charlene Guillot
Cameron, LA

My mom cooked this dish often, especially for New Year's Day. It is comfort food for me, but I doctored it up a bit to be a little healthier.

16-oz. pkg. dried black-eyed
    peas
4 c. vegetable broth
3 c. water
1 lb. smoked pork sausage,
    diced
2 cloves garlic, chopped
1 onion, chopped

1/2 c. celery, chopped
2 c. green, yellow, red and/or
    orange peppers, chopped
2 t. salt
2 t. pepper
2 t. cayenne pepper
2 t. red pepper flakes
Optional: cooked rice

Place beans in a bowl; add enough water to cover. Soak for 5 hours to overnight. Drain; add beans to a 5-quart slow cooker. Add broth, water and remaining ingredients except cooked rice; stir well. Cover and cook on high setting for 4 hours, or until beans are tender. Serve bean mixture spooned over cooked rice, if desired. Makes 10 servings.

For a magical ice wreath, arrange cranberries and pine trimmings in a ring mold. Fill with water and freeze until solid, then pop out of the mold. Hang outdoors from a tree branch with a sturdy ribbon.

Quick Ham & Beans

Jenita Davison
La Plata, MO

On a cold Missouri day, ham & beans with cornbread and fried potatoes equals comfort food for us. This is much quicker than most slow-cooker recipes...I can put it on and go on with other activities, with the bonus of slow-cooked taste!

2 stalks celery, chopped
1/2 c. onion, chopped
2 to 3 t. butter
2 16-oz. cans Great Northern
    beans
1-1/2 c. cooked ham, cubed

1-1/2 c. chicken broth
1/2 t. garlic, minced
salt and pepper to taste
Garnish: chopped onion
cornbread

In a skillet over medium heat, sauté celery and onion in butter. Transfer mixture to a 4 to 5-quart slow cooker. Add undrained beans and remaining ingredients except garnish. Cover and cook on high setting for about one hour, until heated through. Turn to low setting and continue cooking for 2 to 3 hours. More broth may be added if a thinner consistency is desired. Serve with chopped onion and cornbread. Makes 6 servings.

There are always so many tempting treats during the holidays.
Lighten things up by keeping a bowl filled with shiny apples
and pears. They'll double as a pretty centerpiece and as
a healthy, crunchy-sweet snack.

Smoked Sausage & Potatoes

Sandy Barnhart
Sapulpa, OK

The flavor combination in this dish is really good. Serve and listen to the rave reviews from your family & friends.

2 T. butter, divided
2 to 3 T. olive oil, divided
1/2 onion, sliced
3/4 to 1 green pepper, sliced
salt to taste
2 cloves garlic, finely chopped

5 to 6 potatoes, peeled and
  thinly sliced
14-oz. pkg. smoked pork
  sausage, thinly sliced
seasoning salt and pepper
  to taste

In a deep skillet over medium heat, melt one tablespoon butter with one tablespoon oil. Add onion, green pepper and a little salt; cook until almost crisp-tender. Add garlic; cook for one to 2 minutes. Remove onion mixture to a plate; add remaining butter and oil to skillet. Add potatoes; cook until tender and golden. Remove potatoes to a separate plate. If desired, add a little more oil to the skillet and sauté sausage 5 to 7 minutes. Combine all ingredients back into skillet; mix together and heat through. Add seasonings to taste. Makes 4 servings.

Give your home a spicy holiday scent year 'round. Cover oranges with whole cloves, piercing the peel in circle and swirl designs or simply covering the fruit at random. Roll in cinnamon and ginger, then stack in a wooden bowl.

Connecticut Supper

Bethi Hendrickson
Danville, PA

This dish always reminds me of those farm suppers as a child with our whole family. Lots of laughing and stories, and then everyone getting up to go to the barn for the evening milking. It is truly a farmer-type dish.

1 lb. ground beef
4 potatoes, peeled and thinly
   sliced
10-3/4 oz. can cream of
   mushroom soup
2-1/4 c. milk

1 t. salt
1 c. sharp Cheddar cheese,
   shredded
1/4 c. Italian-flavored dry bread
   crumbs
2 T. butter, melted

Brown beef in a skillet over medium heat; drain. Transfer beef to a greased 13"x9" baking pan. Arrange potato slices over beef; set aside. In a small saucepan over medium heat, combine soup, milk and salt. Cook and stir until creamy and heated through. Spoon soup mixture over potatoes. Evenly layer cheese over the top. In a small bowl, combine bread crumbs and melted butter. Toss with a fork until mixed well; sprinkle over cheese. Bake, uncovered, at 350 degrees for 1-1/2 hours. Makes 4 to 6 servings.

For a warm, cozy holiday fragrance, simmer cinnamon sticks, citrus peel, whole cloves and nutmeg in a mini slow cooker. Just add 2 to 3 cups of water and set on low. A small saucepan set over low heat on the stovetop works too.

Herbed Stuffed Zucchini

Donna Wilson
Maryville, TN

I love zucchini! I found this recipe years ago, and it has been a favorite of mine ever since.

4 zucchini, halved lengthwise
2 T. tomato paste
1/4 t. dried basil
1/4 t. dried oregano

1 clove garlic, minced
1/4 c. dry bread crumbs
1/2 to 1 c. shredded mozzarella
  cheese

Scoop pulp out of each zucchini half; set aside. Place zucchini shells cut-side down in a large skillet; add 1/2 inch boiling water. Cover; simmer over medium heat until tender. Meanwhile, in a separate saucepan over medium heat, cook reserved pulp, tomato paste, herbs and garlic until mixture comes to a boil. Spoon mixture into zucchini shells; sprinkle with bread crumbs and cheese. Place on a broiler pan; broil until cheese melts. Serves 4 to 6.

Rosemary Roasted Acorn Squash

Beckie Langford
Tappahannock, VA

This recipe is good for all kinds of autumn squash... super-sweet acorn squash is my favorite.

1 acorn squash, peeled and
  cut into 1-inch cubes
2 T. olive oil
1/2 t. dried rosemary

1/2 t. salt-free original
  seasoning
1/2 t. salt
1/2 t. pepper

Place squash cubes on an aluminum foil-lined baking sheet. Add remaining ingredients; toss to coat and arrange in a single layer. Bake at 400 degrees for 20 to 25 minutes, until tender. Serves 4.

Christmas: that magic blanket that wraps itself about us.

–Augusta E. Rundel

Cranberry-Pecan Broccoli Slaw
Lynnette Jones
East Flat Rock, NC

*Dressed with oil & vinegar rather than mayonnaise, this is
a bit healthier version of this potluck favorite. Cranberries
and pecans make it perfect for the holidays!*

2 c. water
3-oz. pkg. chicken-flavored
   ramen noodles
12-oz. pkg. broccoli slaw mix
2 green onions, sliced
1/2 c. celery, diced
1/4 c. chopped pecans

1/4 c. sweetened dried
   cranberries
1/4 c. sugar
2 T. cider vinegar
1/3 c. olive or canola oil
1/2 t. pepper

In a saucepan over high heat, bring water to a boil. Add noodles,
setting aside seasoning packet. Cook for 3 minutes, stirring several
times. Drain and transfer to a serving bowl; allow to cool. Add slaw
mix, green onions, celery, pecans and cranberries; mix gently. In a
separate bowl, combine remaining ingredients and reserved ramen
seasoning. Whisk well; pour over slaw mixture and toss. Cover and
chill. Makes 6 to 8 servings.

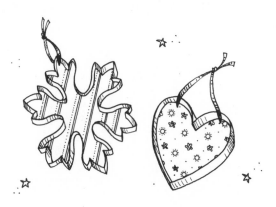

Use thrift-store cookie cutters to make clever tree ornaments...
fun for kids! Choose thick scrapbook paper or color-copy photos
onto cardstock. Trace the cutter's shape on top; cut out paper shape.
Dab craft glue along the cutter's edge. Press paper in place; let dry.
Glue on a piece of ribbon for a hanger.

Sour Cream Spaghetti

Patricia Marzwick
Olympia, WA

My mother-in-law shared this recipe with me. It makes quite a lot, so it's great for a potluck or a gathering of friends. I serve a crisp salad and garlic bread to complete the meal.

10-oz. pkg. medium egg
   noodles, uncooked
2 lbs. ground beef
1 onion, chopped
2 cloves garlic, minced
1 t. sugar
1 t. salt

pepper to taste
2 15-oz. cans tomato sauce
8-oz. pkg. cream cheese,
   softened
16-oz. container sour cream
2 c. shredded Cheddar cheese,
   divided

Cook noodles according to package directions; drain. Meanwhile, brown beef in a large skillet over medium heat; drain. Add onion, garlic, sugar and seasonings to beef; stir in tomato sauce. Simmer over low heat for 15 minutes, stirring occasionally. Add cream cheese and sour cream; mix well. Gently fold in cooked noodles. Layer half of noodle mixture and half of shredded cheese in a greased deep 13"x9" baking pan. Repeat layers. Bake, uncovered, at 350 degrees for 35 to 45 minutes, until bubbly and cheese is melted. Makes 8 to 10 servings.

Perhaps this year, one of Santa's elves will make an appearance in your home! Set out an elf figurine the day after Thanksgiving to "monitor" good behavior. At night, the elf reports back to the North Pole (or so you tell the kids!). Next morning he will be found sitting in a different spot.

Swedish Meatballs

Andrea Heyart
Savannah, TX

*A family favorite, these meatballs have graced our plates
more often than burgers & fries. I can make this dinner
with my eyes closed and it will still turn out perfectly.*

1 egg, beaten
1 c. seasoned dry bread crumbs
1/2 t. salt
1/4 t. pepper
1 lb. ground beef
1/2 to 1 c. oil
2 T. butter
2 T. all-purpose flour

1 c. beef broth
1 t. Worcestershire sauce
2 t. paprika
1 t. garlic powder
salt and pepper to taste
1 c. sour cream
16-oz. pkg. wide egg noodles,
    cooked

In a large bowl, combine egg, bread crumbs, seasonings and beef.
Mix well; form into small meatballs. Heat oil in a skillet over medium
heat, adding enough oil to come 1/3 up the side of meatballs. Add
meatballs; cook until browned and cooked through. Drain meatballs
on paper towels; set aside. Melt butter in a large saucepan over
medium heat. Sprinkle in flour; cook and stir to form a thick brown
paste. Whisk in broth; cook and stir until mixture just begins to
thicken. Add Worcestershire sauce, seasonings and sour cream; mix
well. Bring mixture to a simmer over medium heat, stirring often. Add
meatballs; cover and simmer over low heat for at least 15 minutes.
Serve meatballs and sauce over cooked noodles. Makes 4 to 6 servings.

Fill a big glass jar with vintage-style candies...guests of all ages
will love scooping out their favorites!

Quick & Easy Chili Mac

Joanna Wright
Orange, TX

This is a quick kid-friendly meal, perfect for busy weeknights.
My grandchildren love to tell you how to make MawMaw's
chili mac. We love it with fresh-baked buttered cornbread muffins.

7-oz. pkg. macaroni & cheese
   mix
1 lb. ground beef
1 onion, chopped

1/2 green pepper, chopped
2 15-oz. cans ranch-style beans
chili powder, salt and pepper
   to taste

Cook macaroni from mix according to package directions; drain.
Meanwhile, in a skillet over medium heat, brown beef with onion and
green pepper; drain. Add beans and cooked macaroni to beef mixture.
Sprinkle with cheese powder from mix; add seasonings and stir well.
Makes 6 servings.

Share the Christmas spirit with a good winter deed...shovel the
driveway and sidewalk for a neighbor. When you reach the doorstep,
be sure to knock on the door and wish them a merry Christmas!

Cheesy Chicken Casserole

Cindy Joseph
Barrington, RI

This is an easy, delicious slow-cooker recipe...great for cold nights.

6 boneless, skinless chicken
　breasts
1 c. shredded Cheddar cheese
10-3/4 oz. can cream of
　mushroom soup

1/4 c. milk
6-oz. pkg. herb-flavored stuffing
　mix
1/2 c. butter, melted

Spray a 5 to 6-quart slow cooker with non-stick vegetable spray. Layer chicken in crock; top with cheese. Whisk together soup and milk in a bowl; spoon over cheese. Sprinkle dry stuffing on top; drizzle with melted butter. Cover and cook on low setting for 8 to 10 hours, or on high setting for 4 to 6 hours. Makes 6 servings.

A special memory from long ago. It was my first year in college,
and I was living with my grandmother. Many uncles, aunts and
cousins lived nearby. My aunt had bought a horse and I was happy
to help put up fencing across a large field. One day I realized I had
lost my high school ring, somewhere in a vast expanse of grass.
I searched and searched for it, to no avail, gave up and considered
it lost. On Christmas Eve, we had a huge family celebration, well over
75 people, and there was a small gift for everyone from my sweet
Nana. After all the gifts were opened, I received another small box
from "Santa." I was bewildered, because I was the only one to receive
this extra gift. Imagine my shock when I opened the box and found
my ring! I could not believe my eyes; how had this happened? Finally
my dear Uncle Allan smiled and said that he had gone out with
his metal detector and found the ring for me. The gift of his love
and time was one of the most special gifts I ever received. I treasured
the ring even more because he passed away a few years later,
at a very young age. Truly, caring for others is the best way
to celebrate the love that is Christmas!

–Faye Kepner, Sunderland, MD

Pink Party Pasta

Cyndy DeStefano
Mercer, PA

This tomato-flavored pasta is great to serve company! It tastes so good, is so pretty in a big pasta bowl, and your guests will never guess how easy it is to make

16-oz. pkg. favorite pasta, uncooked
2 T. butter, sliced
1 T. olive oil
4 cloves garlic, finely minced

24-oz. jar tomato-basil pasta sauce
1 c. whipping cream
Garnish: chopped fresh basil

Cook pasta as package directs; drain. Meanwhile, melt butter with oil in a deep skillet over medium heat. Add garlic; sauté just until lightly golden. Add sauce to skillet; cook and stir well until heated through. Reduce heat to low; stir in cream. Ladle sauce over cooked pasta in a serving bowl; sprinkle with basil. Serves 6.

Garlic & Parsley Pasta Toss

April Jacobs
Loveland, CO

Need a simple side in a jiffy? This is tasty and so easy!

12-oz. pkg. angel hair pasta, uncooked
2 t. garlic, minced
1 to 2 T. olive oil
1/2 c. water

2 cubes chicken bouillon
1/2 c. fresh parsley, chopped
Garnish: grated Parmesan cheese

Cook pasta as package directs; drain. Meanwhile, in a small skillet over medium heat, cook garlic in oil until golden. Add water and bouillon; cook and stir until bouillon dissolves. In a large bowl, toss cooked pasta with garlic mixture and parsley. Serve with Parmesan cheese. Serves 4 to 6.

Spinach Parmesan Orzo

Kathleen Sturm
Corona, CA

This easy side dish is excellent...everyone I have made it for loves it! I like to sauté the spinach early in the day so it's a bit quicker to prepare at dinnertime.

4 T. butter, divided
1 T. garlic, chopped
6-oz. pkg. fresh baby spinach
1/8 t. salt
1 c. orzo pasta, uncooked

14-1/2 oz. can chicken broth
1/2 c. shredded Parmesan or
    Italian-blend cheese
salt and pepper to taste

Melt 2 tablespoons butter in a large skillet over medium heat. Add garlic; sauté for about 30 seconds, just until lightly golden. Add spinach and salt to skillet. Sauté for a few minutes until spinach is wilted; set aside spinach in a bowl. In the same skillet, melt remaining butter over medium-high heat. Add uncooked pasta; cook and stir until lightly golden. Stir in broth. Reduce heat to low; cover and simmer until orzo is cooked and liquid is almost gone, 10 to 15 minutes. Remove from heat. Add wilted spinach and cheese; toss to combine. Season with salt and pepper. Serves 6 to 8.

To keep a potted Christmas poinsettia fresh, place it in a sunny spot, away from cold drafts. Water whenever the soil on top feels dry.

Creamed Turkey

Janis Parr
Ontario, Canada

This is a great way to use up the leftover turkey from Christmas dinner. I also crumble a little of the leftover stuffing on each serving and place a spoonful of cranberry sauce on the side. Comfort food at its best!

6 T. butter	1-1/2 c. turkey or chicken broth
6 T. all-purpose flour	4 c. cooked turkey, diced
1 t. salt	1 c. celery, chopped
1/8 t. pepper	1 egg yolk, beaten
1-1/2 c. milk, warmed	6 to 8 biscuits, split and buttered

Melt butter in a large saucepan over medium heat. Sprinkle with flour, salt and pepper; blend well. Add warm milk and broth; cook and stir over medium heat until thickened. Add turkey, celery and egg yolk. Cover and cook on low heat for 20 minutes, stirring occasionally. To serve, ladle turkey mixture over split, buttered biscuits. Makes 6 to 8 servings.

Remember pets at Christmas...they're family too! Trim a whimsical Christmas tree or wreath with kitten figurines, tiny catnip mice and strands of yarn, or puppy figurines, dog treats and garlands of leash webbing.

Turkey on the Run

Brenda Len
Georgetown, TX

This recipe is one I created years ago from what I had on hand. It was such a hit, my family asked for it regularly.

1 lb. ground turkey
1 t. garlic powder
1 t. onion powder
1 t. dried cumin
1/2 t. kosher salt, or more to
  taste
1/2 t. pepper
1-1/2 c. frozen cut green beans

1-1/2 c. frozen corn
16-oz. can black beans, drained
  and rinsed
1 c. beef broth
2/3 c. orzo pasta, uncooked
1/2 c. shredded mozzarella
  cheese
1/2 c. shredded Cheddar cheese

Brown turkey in a large non-stick skillet over medium-high heat. Drain; sprinkle with seasonings. Add frozen vegetables and black beans; sauté until heated through, 5 to 10 minutes. Stir in broth and uncooked orzo; bring to a boil. Reduce heat to medium-low. Cover and simmer for about 10 minutes, until orzo is nearly tender. Simmer, uncovered, until most of liquid has evaporated. Remove from heat. Top with cheeses; cover and let stand until cheeses melt. Makes 4 to 6 servings.

Wrap and freeze small amounts of leftover cheeses. They may become crumbly when thawed, but will still be delicious in casseroles and one-dish dinners.

Grammy's Pea Salad

Rebecca Gonzalez
Moreno Valley, CA

*My mom always made this simple salad when I was growing up,
it was always my favorite. Now Mom is known as Grammy
around my house and she still makes our favorite salad.*

15-oz. can peas, drained
15-oz. can corn, drained
15-oz. can kidney beans,
   drained and rinsed

4-1/2 oz. jar sliced mushrooms,
   drained
2 green onions, chopped
1/4 c. mayonnaise

Combine all vegetables in a serving bowl; toss to mix. Add mayonnaise;
stir until coated well. Cover and chill for one hour before serving.
Serves 4 to 6.

One late December, it was funny how all of a sudden we kids weren't
asked to bring in groceries from the trunk anymore. In the past, my
sister Terri and I had found Christmas presents and had even played
with them for a month. That year we had asked for beanbag chairs.
We really wanted those beanbag chairs! Hers would be blue and
mine green to match our rooms. Christmas Eve night, after going to
Grandmaw's house and church, we were sent to bed. I woke up in
the middle of the night and could hear something being dragged.
I looked down the long hall and there was Dad dragging two beanbag
chairs into the living room. I could barely contain myself! How I
ever went back to sleep I don't know, but when 6 a.m. arrived,
I was at the Christmas tree, sitting in my green beanbag chair.
What a great Christmas!

–Lori Fresina, Ponchatoula, LA

Merry Christmas

Feasts

Bacon-Wrapped Pork Tenderloin

Sue Klapper
Muskego, WI

This is one of our favorite Christmas Day meals. My cousin and I take turns hosting Christmas dinner. When it's my turn, I like to do something a little different. The pork is so tender and delicious, and it is very easy to prepare.

1 T. garlic powder	1/2 t. dried oregano
1 t. dried basil	2-lb. pork tenderloin, trimmed
1 t. seasoned salt	3 slices bacon
1 t. pepper	1 to 2 T. olive oil

Combine seasonings in a cup. Mix well; rub all over tenderloin. Wrap tenderloin with bacon; secure with wooden toothpicks. Coat well with oil; place in an ungreased 13"x9" baking pan. Bake, uncovered, at 375 degrees for 45 to 60 minutes, until bacon is crisp and thickest part of tenderloin reaches 145 to 155 degrees on a meat thermometer. Remove from oven; wrap tenderloin in aluminum foil. Let stand for 10 minutes before slicing. Serves 4.

For Christmas, my husband, our daughters and I pick out 23 books from the girls' bookshelf. Together we wrap them up and the girls put a number on each book. Then we put the books in a special place by the Christmas tree. Every night in December, the girls unwrap the book for that day and we read it together as a family. Then on Christmas Eve we read "The Night Before Christmas." Our girls, aged five and six, are more excited about this tradition than about getting gifts.

–Kat Beumer, Hockley, TX

Carefree Company Chicken
Cindy Cleland
British Columbia, Canada

This is a family favorite. The aroma is sure to make your mouth water, and keep you coming into the kitchen asking, "Is dinner done yet?" Quick and simple never tasted so yummy!

4 to 6 boneless, skinless chicken breasts, whole or cubed
10-3/4 oz. can cream of mushroom soup
8-oz. container sour cream

1-oz. pkg. onion soup mix
2 T. cooking sherry or chicken broth
1 t. dill seed

Arrange chicken in a buttered 3-quart casserole dish. Combine remaining ingredients in a bowl; mix well and spoon over chicken. Bake, uncovered, at 350 degrees for one to 1-1/4 hours, until bubbly and chicken juices run clear when pierced. Makes 4 servings.

Make it easy on yourself when planning holiday dinners...stick to tried & true recipes! You'll find your guests are just as happy with simple comfort foods as with the most elegant gourmet meal.

Ethel's 4-Cheese Lasagna

Carol Ferryman
Urbana, OH

My mother-in-law would make this easy recipe for
Sunday dinners. Always so good!

8-oz. pkg. wide egg noodles,
    uncooked
1 lb. ground beef
1/2 onion, chopped
minced garlic or garlic powder
    to taste
1-3/4 c. tomato juice
6-oz. can tomato paste
1/4 c. sugar

1/2 to 1 t. dried oregano
salt and pepper to taste
8-oz. pkg. shredded Cheddar
    cheese
8-oz. pkg. shredded Swiss
    cheese
12-oz. container cottage cheese
1 c. grated Parmesan cheese

Cook noodles according to package directions; drain. Meanwhile, in a large skillet over medium heat, cook beef, onion and garlic; drain. Stir in tomato juice, tomato paste, sugar and seasonings. Reduce heat to low; simmer for 20 minutes, stirring occasionally. Combine beef mixture and cooked noodles in a large bowl; stir very well. Add shredded cheeses and cottage cheese; mix well. Spoon into a 13"x9" baking pan sprayed with non-stick vegetable spray. Top with Parmesan cheese. Bake, uncovered, at 350 degrees for 30 minutes, or until bubbly and cheeses are melted. Makes 6 to 8 servings.

Pick up one or two table settings of a different holiday pattern each year. Before long, you'll have a collection of delightfully mismatched dishes and special memories to go with each.

Linguine & Artichokes in White Sauce

*Annette Ceravolo
Hoover, AL*

I have used this meatless recipe for many years, especially during Lent. Changed a few things to make easier without losing the flavor. I like to serve it with a zesty tossed salad.

16-oz. pkg. linguine pasta,
   uncooked
5 T. butter, sliced
6 T. extra-virgin olive oil
1 t. all-purpose flour
1 c. chicken broth
1 clove garlic, pressed
2 t. lemon juice
1 t. fresh parsley, minced

salt and pepper to taste
14-oz. can quartered artichoke
   hearts, drained
3 T. grated Parmesan cheese
1 to 2 t. small capers, drained
   and rinsed
Garnish: additional grated
   Parmesan cheese

Cook pasta according to package directions; drain. Meanwhile, in a large heavy skillet, melt butter with oil over low heat. Sprinkle with flour; cook and stir for 3 minutes. Increase heat to medium-high. Stir in broth; cook for one minute. Add garlic, lemon juice, parsley, salt and pepper; simmer over low heat for 5 minutes, stirring occasionally. Add artichokes, Parmesan cheese and capers; cover and simmer for 8 minutes. In a large serving dish, combine cooked pasta and artichoke mixture; toss together until well coated with sauce. Divide among 4 plates; top each with additional cheese. Makes 4 servings.

Make mini wreaths of pine-scented rosemary to slip around dinner napkins. Simply wind fresh rosemary stems into a ring shape, tuck in the ends and tie on a tiny bow...so festive!

Mom's Barbecue Brisket

LaShelle Brown
Mulvane, KS

Every year my family gets together on Christmas Eve for dinner and this is always on the menu. A true family favorite!

2 c. favorite barbecue sauce, divided
2 T. smoke-flavored cooking sauce
2 t. Worcestershire sauce
2 t. celery seed
1 t. garlic salt
1 t. onion salt
2 t. pepper
4-lb. beef brisket

In a small bowl, mix together one cup barbecue sauce, remaining sauces and seasonings. Spread over both sides of brisket. Place brisket in a plastic zipping bag; seal bag and refrigerate overnight. When ready to cook, place brisket in an ungreased 13"x9" baking pan. Cover very tightly with aluminum foil, creasing the foil to cover as tightly as possible and prevent liquid from evaporating. Bake at 300 degrees for 4 hours, checking occasionally to be certain foil is still in place. Uncover; spread remaining barbecue sauce over brisket. Bake, uncovered, for another 45 minutes to one hour, until fork-tender. Remove brisket to a platter; let stand 10 minutes and slice on the diagonal. Makes 10 to 12 servings.

Be sure to share your family's stories behind the special foods that are a tradition at every holiday dinner... Grandmother's green beans, Aunt Jessie's famous walnut cake, Mom's secret seasoning for the roast beef. There may even be stories to tell about the whimsical salt & pepper shakers!

Grandma's Calico Baked Beans
Julie Harris
Boiling Springs, SC

I have fond memories of helping my grandma make this delicious dish the night before a church potluck. She would tie one of her big aprons on me and roll up my sleeves, so I could help make the sauce. As a newlywed I now make this for my own family and our church potlucks, and I am always reminded of those special times helping Grandma in the kitchen.

1/2 lb. bacon, diced
1 lb. ground beef
1/2 c. onion, chopped
1 clove garlic, minced
1/2 c. brown sugar, packed
1/2 c. catsup
1/4 c. water
1 T. cider vinegar
1 t. salt
1 t. mustard
Optional: 1/8 t. smoke-flavored
   cooking sauce
21-oz. can pork & beans
16-oz. can kidney beans,
   drained and rinsed
16-oz. can Great Northern
   beans, drained and rinsed

In a large skillet, cook bacon over medium heat until crisp. Remove bacon to paper towels; discard drippings. In the same skillet, brown beef, onion and garlic; drain. In a large bowl, whisk together brown sugar, catsup, water, vinegar, salt, mustard and sauce, if using. Add beans, crumbled bacon and beef mixture; stir well. Spoon mixture into a greased 2-quart casserole dish. Bake, uncovered, at 325 degrees for 45 to 60 minutes, until beans are bubbly and as thick as desired. May also be cooked in a slow cooker. Cover and cook on high setting for 2 to 3 hours, or on low setting for 5 to 6 hours. Makes 10 to 15 servings.

An old-fashioned bean pot becomes a perfect gift when filled with packages of assorted dried beans and a tried & true recipe for baked beans.

Golden Lemony Baked Chicken

Amanda Johnson
Marysville, OH

This chicken is one of my family's absolute favorites. We love it with split chicken breasts, but you could use legs and thighs as well.

1/2 c. olive oil, divided
4 chicken breasts
4 to 5 cloves garlic, pressed

4 lemons, halved
dried parsley, salt and pepper
  to taste

Coat the bottom of a 13"x9" baking pan with 1/4 cup oil. Arrange chicken in pan skin-side up; drizzle with remaining oil. Coat chicken evenly with garlic. Squeeze lemon juice over chicken; place lemon halves in pan with chicken. Bake, uncovered, at 375 degrees for one to 1-1/2 hours, until chicken juices run clear when pierced. Makes 4 servings.

At last the dinner was all done, the cloth was cleaned,
the hearth swept and the fire made up.
A Merry Christmas to us all, my dears.
God bless us! Which all the family re-echoed,
God bless us every one.

–Charles Dickens

Merry Christmas
Feasts

Simple Cranberry Turkey Breast

Diane Smith
Burlington, NJ

Enjoy the flavors of the holidays anytime without cooking a huge meal! Just put your slow cooker to work. The sauce created from the turkey breast cooking can be used as a gravy for the sliced meat or combined with bread cubes to make a dressing side dish.

6 to 8-lb. turkey breast
15-oz. can whole-berry
   cranberry sauce

1-oz. pkg. onion soup mix
14-oz. can chicken broth

Spray a 6 to 7-quart slow cooker with non-stick vegetable spray. Place turkey breast into crock and set aside. Combine cranberry sauce and soup mix in a small bowl; stir until well combined and spread over turkey. Pour broth over turkey. Cover and cook on low setting for 7 hours, or until turkey is very tender. Remove turkey to a platter; let stand several minutes before slicing. Serves 8 to 10.

Put stemmed glasses to use as candle holders...simply turn them
over, placing a shiny ornament ball underneath. Top each with
a short pillar candle. Group several together on a tray for
a table decoration that's done in a snap.

147

Christmas Comfort Classics

Pineapple Beets

Elizabeth Smithson
Cunningham, KY

I found this recipe in a farm cookbook years age. Hadn't used it in a while...no one but me would eat beets! I thought of this when I needed to take a dish to a homemakers' meeting...it was a hit!

8-oz. can pineapple tidbits
2 T. brown sugar, packed
1 T. cornstarch
1/4 t. salt

1 T. butter
1 T. lemon juice
16-oz. can sliced beets, drained

In a saucepan, combine pineapple with juice, brown sugar, cornstarch and salt. Bring to a boil, stirring constantly, until thickened, about 2 minutes. Stir in butter and lemon juice; add beets. Cook over medium heat for 5 minutes, stirring occasionally. Makes 4 servings.

Honey-Glazed Carrots

Marsha Baker
Pioneer, OH

When it's a busy day, this slow-cooker recipe is great to put on in the afternoon. It'll be ready when you are.

1 lb. carrots, peeled and cut into
  1-inch pieces, or 1 lb. baby
  carrots

2 T. butter, melted
2 T. honey or agave nectar
salt and pepper to taste

Spray a 2 to 3-quart slow cooker with non-stick vegetable spray. Add carrots; drizzle with butter and honey or nectar. Season with salt and pepper. Cover and cook on high setting for 2-1/2 to 3 hours, until carrots are tender and glazed. Serves 4 to 6.

It is Christmas in the heart that puts
Christmas in the air.

–W.T. Ellis

Slow-Cooked Green Beans

Rita Frye
King, NC

This recipe is very forgiving. I haven't used exact measures since I was a bride, many years ago! But these are the instructions I've given to my stepdaughters when they were brides, and their husbands are certainly well-fed. I usually prepare it for Sunday dinner. If a crowd is coming, I increase everything except the onions.

2 to 3 14-1/2 oz. cans green
   beans, drained
4-oz. can sliced mushrooms,
   drained

8-oz. jar pearl onions, drained
1/4 c. brown sugar, packed
1/4 c. butter, sliced

Combine green beans, mushrooms and onions in a 4-quart slow cooker; stir gently. Sprinkle with brown sugar; dot with butter. Cover and cook on low setting for 3 hours, until bubbly and glazed. Makes 6 servings.

The more the merrier! Why not invite a neighbor or a college student who might be spending the holiday alone to share in the Christmas feast?

Marinated Beef Tenderloin

Karen Wilson
Defiance, OH

*This is the recipe my mom served for Christmas
and other special holidays.*

4 to 6-lb. beef tenderloin,
  trimmed
1-1/2 c. water
1 c. catsup

2 .7-oz. pkgs. Italian salad
  dressing mix
2 t. mustard
1 t. Worcestershire sauce

Pierce tenderloin in several places with a fork. Place in a large plastic
zipping bag; set aside. In a small bowl, combine remaining ingredients;
mix well. Reserve and refrigerate 1/2 cup marinade. Pour remaining
marinade over tenderloin in bag. Seal bag and refrigerate for 8 hours,
turning occasionally. Remove tenderloin, discarding marinade in bag.
Place on a wire rack in a roasting pan. Bake, uncovered at 425 degrees
for 45 to 50 minutes, brushing with reserved marinade 3 to 4 times.
Tenderloin is done when a meat thermometer reads 140 degrees
for rare, 150 degrees for medium-rare, 160 degrees for medium or
170 degrees for well-done. Remove to a platter; let stand several
minutes before slicing. Serves 8 to 12.

Set a festive table with items you
already have! Green transferware
serving bowls and jadite cake
stands, sparkling white porcelain
dinner plates and ruby-red stemmed
glasses combine beautifully with
Christmas dinnerware.

Easy Popovers

Nancy Triezenberg
Palos Park, IL

My mother used to work so hard making Yorkshire Pudding for every Sunday dinner. When she passed away, no one had the recipe...it was just in her head. My sister had tasted these popovers at a friend's home and loved them, so when I tried them for my family they couldn't get enough of them. They're so easy too.

5 T. butter, melted and divided
1-1/2 c. all-purpose flour
1-1/2 c. whole milk
4 eggs
1/2 t. kosher salt

Brush 12 non-stick muffin cups with 2 tablespoons melted butter; set aside. In a large bowl, whisk together remaining butter and other ingredients until only a few lumps remain. Do not overmix. Divide batter among buttered muffin cups. Bake at 400 degrees for 30 to 35 minutes, until puffed and deeply golden. Do not open oven door before 30 minutes, or popovers will collapse. Remove one popover from the tin to check that the bottom is golden. Serve immediately. Makes one dozen.

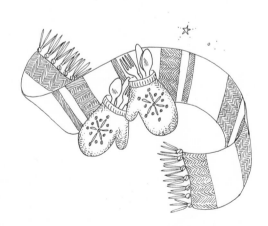

Do you have lots of family members to buy for? Choose a single item like woolly knitted scarves or cozy winter slippers to buy for everyone, in different colors and textures.

Easy Freezer Lasagna

Liz Plotnick-Snay
Gooseberry Patch

In celebration of my 50th birthday, some friends and I got together and made eight trays of lasagna for undernourished moms-to-be in our area. This recipe would also be perfect for taking to a friend who just needed a helping hand! Use a disposable foil pan to freeze.

9 whole-wheat lasagna noodles, uncooked
1 lb. ground turkey
1 onion, chopped
1/8 t. garlic powder
24-oz. jar spaghetti sauce
2 c. low-fat cottage cheese
1/4 c. grated Parmesan cheese
2 t. dried parsley
12-oz. pkg. shredded mozzarella cheese
1 handful fresh spinach

Cook noodles as package directs; drain and rinse in cold water. Meanwhile, brown turkey, onion and garlic powder in a skillet over medium heat; drain. Add sauce and simmer over low heat for 15 minutes, stirring occasionally. In a bowl, combine cottage cheese, Parmesan cheese and parsley; mix well. To assemble, spread a small amount of sauce mixture in a 13"x9" baking pan. Layer 1/3 of noodles over sauce in pan, tearing to fit as needed; top with 1/3 of sauce, 1/3 of mozzarella cheese and 1/3 of cottage cheese mixture, dotting spoonfuls over mozzarella. Add all of spinach. Repeat layering twice, except spinach, ending with mozzarella. Cover and bake at 350 degrees for 40 to 45 minutes, until hot and bubbly. Let stand 10 minutes before serving. To freeze, let cool; cover with foil lid and freeze. To bake, thaw frozen lasagna in refrigerator overnight; bake as above. May also bake, still frozen, at 350 degrees for 1-1/2 to 2 hours, until hot and bubbly. Serves 6 to 8.

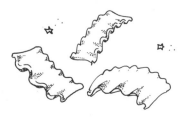

Cooked lasagna noodles are much easier to handle if removed from the pasta pot with tongs, one at a time, and laid flat on a dry tea towel.

Crescent Dinner Rolls

Pieterina Hengstmengel
Alberta, Canada

For Thanksgiving and Christmas get-togethers, it has always been our family's tradition that everyone brings a different type of food to eat. Once I brought these dinner rolls, and now every time they are requested again. They are truly delicious!

3-1/2 to 3-3/4 c. all-purpose
    flour, divided
3/4 c. butter, softened and
    divided
1/4 c. sugar
1 t. salt

1 env. active dry yeast
1/2 c. warm water,
    120 to 130 degrees
1/2 c. warm milk,
    120 to 130 degrees
1 egg, beaten

In a large bowl, combine 2 cups flour, 1/4 cup butter, sugar, salt and yeast; stir until well mixed. Add warm water, warm milk and egg. Beat together with a wooden spoon until smooth. Stir in enough of remaining flour, 1/4 cup at a time, until dough is easy to handle. Place dough onto a lightly floured surface; knead until smooth and elastic. Place dough into a greased bowl, turning once to grease dough on all sides. Cover with a tea towel. Let rise for one hour, or until double in volume. Dough is ready when an indentation remains when touched. Gently push your fist into dough to deflate. Place onto a floured surface; divide dough in half. Melt remaining butter. Roll out each half into a 12-inch circle; brush with some of the melted butter. Cut each circle into 16 wedges. Roll up each wedge, beginning at the widest edge. Place rolls, with points underneath, on lightly greased baking sheets; curve slightly. Brush remaining butter over rolls. Cover with a tea towel; let rise for 30 minutes, or until double. Bake at 350 degrees for 10 to 12 minutes, until lightly golden. Makes about 2-1/2 dozen.

Toss a red & white patterned quilt over the sofa for instant Christmas warmth.

Brined Turkey Breast

Cheryl Sandt
Tallahassee, FL

*This is the juiciest turkey I've ever made! I combined elements
from several recipes to make up the brine for this turkey breast.*

4 c. chicken broth
4 c. apple juice
1/2 c. sea salt
1-1/2 t. dried rosemary
1-1/2 t. dried sage

1-1/2 t. dried thyme
8 c. ice water
8 to 10-lb. turkey breast,
   thawed if frozen

In a stockpot over high heat, combine broth, juice and seasonings.
Bring to a boil; stir until salt is dissolved. Remove from heat. Cool to
room temperature; pour into a food container large enough to hold
turkey and one gallon liquid. Stir in ice water. Place turkey in brine,
breast-side down; be sure entire breast is covered. Cover and refrigerate
for 12 hours. When ready to roast, discard brine. Pat turkey dry and
roast as desired. Serves 8 to 10.

Port Wine Cranberry Dressing

Laura Witham
Anchorage, AK

*One year I was asked to bring the cranberry sauce to my family's
holiday dinner. I just couldn't let myself bring the canned kind,
so I experimented with flavors and found my own new favorite!*

1 c. port wine
1 c. orange juice
3/4 c. water

1-1/2 c. dark brown sugar,
   packed
2 12-oz. pkgs. fresh cranberries

In a large saucepan, combine wine, juice and water. Bring to a boil
over medium-high heat. Immediately turn down to a low boil; stir in
sugar. Add cranberries. Simmer over medium-low heat until sauce is
jam-like, about 25 minutes. Chill and serve. Serves 6 to 8.

Grandmama's Cornbread Dressing

Abigayle Wiseman
Poplar Grove, IL

This recipe is a family favorite that has been handed down through a few generations and saved for special occasions like Thanksgiving and Christmas. To save time on the big day, bake the cornbread and prepare the bread and crackers the night before. Keep covered.

8-1/2 oz. pkg. cornbread mix
6 slices bread, crumbled
1 sleeve saltine crackers,
   crushed
1 onion, diced

6 eggs, beaten
2 14-oz. cans chicken broth
1/2 c. butter, melted
dried sage, salt and pepper
   to taste

Prepare and bake cornbread mix as package directs; cool. Crumble cornbread into a lightly greased 4-quart casserole dish. Add bread and saltines; toss to mix. Add remaining ingredients; mix well. Bake at 350 degrees for 1-1/2 to 2 hours, until thickened and golden on top. Makes 8 to 10 servings.

Grandmother never tossed out day-old bread and neither should you! It keeps its texture better than very fresh bread...it's thrifty too. Cut it into cubes, pack into freezer bags and freeze for making stuffing cubes, casserole toppings and herbed salad croutons.

Family-Favorite Shrimp Creole

Irene Putman
Canal Fulton, OH

*We've been loving this recipe for years! It's always been
a favorite and is as easy to make as it is to eat. Served
with a salad, it makes a great meal for everyone.*

1/2 c. butter
1 c. green pepper, chopped
1 c. green onions, diced
1 c. onion, diced
1 c. celery, diced
2 cloves garlic, minced
2 15-oz. cans diced tomatoes
3 T. tomato paste
2 bay leaves

3 T. cornstarch
2 c. cold water
1 T. lemon juice
1 to 1-1/2 t. salt
1/4 to 1/2 t. pepper
1/2 t. cayenne pepper
2 to 3 lbs. shrimp, peeled,
    cleaned and thawed if frozen
cooked rice

Melt butter in a large skillet over medium heat. Add green pepper,
onions, celery and garlic; sauté for about 5 minutes. Add tomatoes
with juice, tomato paste and bay leaves. Simmer for 15 minutes. In a
cup, dissolve cornstarch in water; add to mixture and simmer about
5 minutes. Add lemon juice and seasonings; simmer for 15 minutes.
Add shrimp and cook until it turns pink, only about 3 to 5 minutes;
do not overcook. Discard bay leaves; serve over cooked rice. Makes
6 to 8 servings.

Keep frozen shrimp on hand for delicious meals and party snacks
anytime. Let it thaw overnight in the fridge, or for a quicker way,
place the frozen shrimp in a colander and run ice-cold water over it.
To avoid mushy shrimp, don't thaw it in the microwave.

Baked Scallops Deluxe

Audrey Stapleford
Merrimack, NH

This my husband's favorite dish, so much so that he won't eat a scallop dinner unless it's mine! It is a mix of various other scallop recipes that I've come across and altered to create this one. Good with wild rice and a buttered, steamed veggie.

1 lb. fresh sea scallops
1/2 c. milk
1 egg, beaten
1 c. buttery round crackers,
    crushed

1/2 c. butter, melted
2 cloves garlic, minced
2 t. fresh dill weed, chopped

Cut large scallops in half; place in a heat-proof bowl. Add enough boiling water to cover; let stand for 3 minutes. Drain; pat dry with paper towels. Dip scallops in milk, then egg, then crushed crackers. Place in a greased 8"x8" baking pan or divide among 4 scallop baking shells. Combine butter and garlic; spoon over scallops. Sprinkle dill and remaining crackers over scallops. Bake, uncovered, at 350 degrees for 15 minutes. Serves 4.

Easy-Peasy Lemon Shrimp

Cyndy DeStefano
Mercer, PA

This is so quick, easy and good enough for company.
Serve over angel hair pasta, if you wish.

1/2 c. butter, melted
1 lemon, sliced
1 lb. medium shrimp, peeled,
    cleaned and thawed,
    if frozen

.7-oz. pkg. Italian salad
    dressing mix

Add butter to a 13"x9" baking pan; place in a 350-degree oven until melted. Remove pan from oven; arrange lemon slices over butter. Arrange shrimp over butter in a single layer. Sprinkle with dressing mix. Bake at 350 degrees for 15 minutes, or until shrimp turns pink. Serves 4.

Southern Pork Barbecue

Lois Jones
LaPorte, IN

We just love this! Barbecue may not seem like a traditional Christmas recipe, but it is one at our house. My guys look forward to this at Christmas, New Year's and throughout the rest of the year. I look forward to making it. We all love it so much and it's been a part of many special meals we've enjoyed together. Many of my son's friends have called before they come to visit us and requested I make it while they are there. I almost always double it so we have some leftovers for several days of extra sandwich making.

6 to 7-lb. pork shoulder, fat and skin trimmed	2 to 3 T. mustard
1 c. white vinegar	1 T. salt
5 T. Worcestershire sauce	1-1/8 t. red pepper flakes
3/8 t. hot pepper sauce, or more to taste	1 t. dried thyme
	12 sandwich buns, split
	Optional: favorite coleslaw

Cut pork from the bone into cubes, one to 2 inches square. Place pork cubes and bone in a large roasting pan; set aside. In a bowl, mix vinegar, sauces, mustard and seasonings. Mix well; pour over pork. Cover with aluminum foil, making sure foil does not touch the pork. Bake at 325 degrees for 2-1/2 hours; do not uncover during cooking time. Remove from oven. Remove pork to a cutting board; pull apart with 2 forks and return to cooking juices in roaster. Slice off any remaining pork from bone; add to roaster. Place roaster on the stovetop. Simmer, uncovered, over low heat for about one hour, until juices are almost gone, stirring occasionally. Watch closely to ensure the juices don't cook off completely. Serve pork on buns, topped with coleslaw, if desired. Makes 12 servings.

Warm sandwich buns for a crowd...easy! Fill a roaster with buns, cover with heavy-duty aluminum foil and cut several slits in the foil. Top with several dampened paper towels and tightly cover with more foil. Bake at 250 degrees for 20 minutes, until hot and steamy.

Grandma Irene's Coleslaw Salad

Jacquelynn Daunce
Lockport, NY

Mom and Grandma Irene worked hard to put our holiday meal on the table. I always wanted to help, so Gram taught me how to make the dressing for the coleslaw. This became my job for many, many, holidays to come. Today, I have fond memories of my mother and grandmother every holiday as I make this for my own family.

1/2 lb. cabbage, shredded	2 to 2-1/2 t. sugar
3/4 c. mayonnaise	3 T. milk
1 T. mustard	salt and pepper to taste

Place cabbage in a serving bowl; set aside. In a small bowl, combine mayonnaise and mustard; blend well. Add 2 teaspoons sugar; blend again. Taste; if not sweet enough, add remaining sugar. Add milk, one tablespoon at a time, blending well after each spoonful. If a thinner dressing is preferred, add a few drops more milk. Season with salt and pepper. Pour dressing over cabbage; mix well. For best flavor, serve immediately, or cover and chill. Makes 8 servings.

For a new spin on a traditional Advent calendar, tuck notes, wrapped candies and games into a stocking garland... a great way to count down the days until Santa's visit!

Beef Bourguignon

Beverley Williams
San Antonio, TX

This is a great recipe for Christmas. Done in the slow cooker, an elegant entree is easy.

2-1/2 lbs. beef round steak, cubed
1/4 c. all-purpose flour
1 to 2 T. butter
1-1/2 c. beef broth
1 c. red wine or beef broth
1/4 c. water

3 slices bacon, crisply cooked and crumbled
salt and pepper to taste
8-oz. pkg. sliced mushrooms
2 carrots, peeled and sliced
1/2 onion, diced
Optional: cooked rice or noodles

Place beef in a plastic zipping bag; add flour. Seal bag and toss to coat; set aside. Melt butter in a skillet over medium-high heat. Brown beef on all sides for 5 to 6 minutes. Transfer beef to a 4 to 5-quart slow cooker. Add broth, wine or broth and water; top with crumbled bacon. Cover and cook on high setting for 4 hours. Season with salt and pepper; add vegetables. Cover and cook an additional hour. Stir gently before serving. Serve over cooked rice or noodles, if desired. Makes 4 servings.

When my children were young, on the Friday after Thanksgiving we would choose four charities to help during Advent, one for each week in December. Each child got to pick a favorite of his or her own. We usually brought small wrapped gifts to a local hospital emergency room for children who were ill or injured during the holidays, donated to a local food cupboard, brought mittens to a mitten tree, helped a cause at our church and decorated a tree or doorway at a senior living housing complex. For a nursing home, we baked cookies and brought vases of single-stem red flowers and greenery for their dinner tables. My children loved doing their part in making someone else's day. Giving always makes you feel great!

–Patti Larche, Victor, NY

Cauliflower Au Gratin

Kathy Storey
Cass City, MI

I've always loved to cook. My children grew up with Mom trying a new recipe every week. Now I enjoy cooking with my young grandchildren.

6 T. butter
1 to 2 cloves garlic, minced
1/4 lb. cooked ham, chopped
1 head cauliflower, broken into
    flowerets
2 T. all-purpose flour

1-1/2 c. whipping cream
1/8 t. salt
pepper to taste
1-1/2 c. shredded Swiss cheese
Optional: 2 to 3 T. fresh parsley,
    chopped

Melt butter in a large skillet over medium heat; sauté garlic and ham for 2 minutes. Add cauliflower; cook just until crisp-tender. Combine flour and cream in a small bowl; add to skillet along with salt and pepper. Stir well. Cook and stir until thickened and bubbly; cook and stir one minute more. Transfer mixture to a 2-quart casserole dish; sprinkle with cheese. Place under a preheated broiler until lightly golden, about 2 to 4 minutes. Sprinkle with parsley, if desired. Serve immediately. Makes 6 to 8 servings.

Trim a doll-size Christmas tree with mini ornaments...it's just the right size for a holiday buffet table. So sweet!

Hearty Baked Rigatoni

Maria Kuhns
Crofton, MD

I've made this easy, delicious dish for my family for many years. It can be made ahead of time, or frozen for a later meal. So convenient at the holidays, satisfying and comforting any time of year. Serve with a zesty tossed salad and hot Italian bread.

2 t. extra-virgin olive oil
1 onion, diced
2 cloves garlic, diced
1 lb. ground beef
1 lb. ground mild Italian
    pork sausage
28-oz. jar meatless spaghetti
    sauce

1/2 t. sugar
2 t. Italian seasoning
1/2 t. salt
1/4 t. pepper
16-oz. pkg. rigatoni pasta,
    uncooked
8-oz. pkg. shredded mozzarella
    cheese

Heat oil in a large skillet over medium heat. Sauté onion and garlic for 5 to 7 minutes, or until softened and onion is translucent. Add beef and sausage. Cook until no longer pink, breaking up any larger pieces; drain. Stir in spaghetti sauce, sugar and seasonings. Simmer over low heat for 20 minutes. Meanwhile, cook pasta according to package directions; drain. Add cooked pasta to beef mixture; stir gently. Transfer mixture to a 13"x9" baking pan coated with non-stick vegetable spray; top with cheese. Bake, uncovered, at 350 degrees for 30 minutes, or until bubbly and cheese is melted. Makes 6 servings.

Make a happiness chain to wind around the tree. Cut strips of colorful paper and have family members write a few words on each strip about something that makes them feel happy. Tape strips together into loops to form a chain. Sure to bring smiles!

Birthday Baked Pasta

Mindy Powell
Saratoga Springs, UT

This is my husband's most-requested dinner! I made it for my mother's 50th birthday party and so I call it my birthday baked pasta. It is my go to-meal to bring to new mothers and also perfect for entertaining! It is easy, meatless, healthy and delicious.

16-oz. pkg. penne rigate pasta,
   uncooked
2 T. garlic, minced
1 T. dried chopped onion
2 T. extra-virgin olive oil
2 14-1/2 oz. cans Italian-
   seasoned diced tomatoes
2 T. brown sugar, packed

1 t. Italian seasoning
salt and pepper to taste
10 to 12 fresh basil leaves,
   thinly sliced
2 c. ricotta cheese
3/4 lb. mozzarella cheese,
   thinly sliced

Cook pasta according to package directions, just until tender; drain and return to cooking pot. Meanwhile, in a skillet over medium heat, sauté garlic and onion in oil. Stir in tomatoes with juice; use a potato masher to crush tomatoes. Stir in brown sugar, Italian seasoning, salt and pepper. Simmer for 5 to 10 minutes; stir in basil and turn off heat. Add ricotta cheese to the hot pasta pot; toss to mix. Pour half of sauce into a lightly greased 13"x9" baking pan. Add all of pasta mixture; top with remaining sauce. Top with mozzarella cheese. Bake, uncovered, at 400 degrees for about 15 to 20 minutes, until bubbly and golden on top. Makes 8 servings.

Remember the true meaning of Christmas. Set out a creche with sturdy nativity figures for your kids to add, one per day, leading up to Baby Jesus on Christmas Day.

Mimie's Homestyle Meatballs

Beckie Apple
Grannis, AR

My grandparents were very active in Christian organizations when I was growing up. Very often Mimie would take a covered dish to meetings. My brother and I were fortunate to be allowed to go along on some of these meetings and enjoy all the wonderful food. I remember Mimie's meatballs were always one of our favorites.

2 lbs. ground beef chuck
2 eggs, beaten
3 T. mayonnaise
2 T. onion, finely chopped
1 T. green pepper, finely
   chopped
1/2 t. salt

1/2 t. pepper
1/8 t. garlic powder
1 sleeve round buttery crackers,
   crushed
10-3/4 oz. can cream of
   mushroom soup
1 c. milk

In a large bowl, combine all ingredients except soup and milk. Mix well; form into 2-inch meatballs. Place meatballs in a 13"x9" baking pan sprayed with non-stick vegetable spray. Whisk together soup and milk in a microwave-safe dish. Microwave until hot; beat until smooth and pour over meatballs. Cover pan with aluminum foil. Bake at 375 degrees for 30 minutes. Remove foil and continue baking for 20 minutes, until heated through. Makes 8 servings.

Making lots of meatballs? Grab a cookie scoop and
start scooping...you'll be done in record time!

Nancy's Macaroni & Cheese, Please

Nancy Musgrave
Newbury, VT

My husband loves this mac & cheese so much, he shared the recipe with all the volunteer firemen's wives. We like sharp Vermont Cheddar, of course. Great for a potluck, church supper or whenever you need comfort food. And it tastes even better the next day!

4 T. butter, softened and divided
16-oz. pkg. elbow macaroni,
    uncooked
2 c. cottage cheese
3-1/2 c. milk
1 t. dry mustard
1/8 t. cayenne pepper
1/8 t. nutmeg

1/4 to 1/2 t. salt
1/4 to 1/2 t. pepper
2 to 3 8-oz. pkgs. shredded
    extra sharp Cheddar cheese,
    divided
Garnish: paprika
Optional: bread crumbs,
    melted butter

Coat a 13"x9" baking pan with 2 tablespoons butter; set aside. Place uncooked macaroni in a large bowl; set aside. In a blender, working in batches if necessary, combine cottage cheese, milk, seasonings and half of the shredded cheese. Purée for one minute. Pour blender mixture over macaroni; stir to coat and pour into baking pan. Cover tightly with aluminum foil, sealing around the edges. Place pan on oven rack in the upper third of the oven. Bake at 375 degrees for 30 minutes. Uncover; spread remaining shredded cheese on top and add a sprinkle of paprika. If a crunchy topping is desired, toss bread crumbs with melted butter; sprinkle over casserole. Bake, uncovered, for another 30 minutes. Turn off the oven and let stand 15 minutes, until golden on top. Serves 8.

As much fun as when you were a kid...buy new jammies for everyone spending Christmas Eve at your home!

Nina's Corn Pudding

Melissa Dattoli
Richmond, VA

As far back as I can remember, my mom has always made the best corn pudding! Not too runny and not too stiff. It's great for family get-togethers and the holidays wouldn't be the same without it.

3 eggs, beaten
1/4 c. all-purpose flour
1/2 t. salt
6 T. sugar
3 T. butter, melted and cooled
    slightly

1 T. vanilla extract
15-oz. can corn
15-oz. creamed corn
1 c. milk

In a bowl, combine all ingredients in order listed; mix well. Pour into a greased 8"x8" baking pan. Bake, uncovered, at 375 degrees for one hour, or until center is just set. Remove from oven; let stand for 10 minutes before serving. Makes 10 servings.

One year, I was living away from my family and came home for Christmas. After we opened our presents and cleaned up the wrappings, it was time to start getting dinner ready. My sister Bev looked at me and said, "Where is the ham?" I looked at her and said, "You were supposed to get it" and she said, "No, you were!" As you can guess, we had nothing for Christmas dinner. Living in a small town, there were no restaurants open except the Burger King at the bus station. Yes, our most memorable Christmas dinner was at Burger King! Other dinners, we can't remember, but we will never forget to make sure who has the ham so we don't have to eat fast food again. So, I guess we can say "Thank you" to all those traveling on Greyhound that day, for sharing Christmas dinner with us!

–Annette Moon, Cary, NC

Festive Broccoli Salad

Linda Trammell
Locust Grove, AR

After I came across this recipe at a family gathering, I began making it for our Thanksgiving and Christmas dinners. My son always requests this yummy salad. I am excited to be able to continue this tradition for my daughter's twins grandbabies, Elizabeth and Noah.

8-oz. pkg. shredded mild
    Cheddar cheese
1 bunch broccoli, finely chopped

1 red onion, finely chopped
3-oz. jar bacon bits

Combine cheese, broccoli and onion in a large serving bowl; toss to mix. Add Dressing; mix again. Cover and refrigerate. Add bacon bits at serving time. Makes 6 servings.

Dressing:

3/4 c. mayonnaise
1/4 c. sugar

2 t. cider vinegar

Up to 24 hours ahead, combine vinegar, sugar, mayonnaise together in a small bowl. Mix well; cover and refrigerate.

Make snow ice cream! Whip one cup heavy cream, stir in vanilla extract and sugar to taste, then add 4 cups of freshly fallen snow...so yummy!

Teriyaki Orange Roast Chicken

*Laurie Rupsis
Aiken, SC*

*I don't know where I found this recipe, but I'm glad
I did! It has become my go-to special dish.*

3-1/2 lb. roasting chicken
3/4 c. teriyaki sauce
1/4 c. orange juice
1/4 c. orange marmalade
2 T. olive oil
6 cloves garlic, finely sliced

1/2 lb. green beans, trimmed
6 green onions, green part only,
   cut into large pieces
2 bay leaves
3 large pieces orange zest,
   white pith removed

Pat chicken dry. Tuck wings under and tie legs together with kitchen twine; set aside. In a small bowl, combine teriyaki sauce, orange juice and orange marmalade; set aside. Heat oil in a Dutch oven over medium-high heat. Add garlic; sauté for 2 minutes. Add beans and onions. Cook for 4 minutes, stirring often. Remove pan from heat; push vegetables to one side. Add chicken to pan; brush thoroughly with sauce mixture. Add bay leaves and orange zest to pan. Bake, uncovered, at 375 degrees for about one hour, basting with sauce every 15 minutes, until chicken juices run clear when pierced. Check for doneness after one hour. Turn off oven; allow chicken to rest in oven with the door slightly open for about 15 minutes. Discard bay leaves and zest. Carve chicken; serve with beans and onions. Makes 6 to 8 servings.

When roasting a chicken, make a "rack" for it by layering carrot
and celery sticks in the bottom of the roaster. Not only will the
veggies hold the chicken up out of the pan juices, the juices
will be extra flavorful for making gravy afterwards.

Wild Rice Hot Dish

Lisa Seckora
Eau Claire, WI

*When you get busy with the holidays, this savory casserole
is perfect for everyday or unexpected guests.*

1/2 c. butter
1 c. sliced mushrooms
1/2 c. onions, diced
1 clove garlic, minced
Optional: 1/2 c. chopped pecans

1 c. wild rice, rinsed, drained
   and uncooked
3 c. chicken broth
salt and pepper to taste

Melt butter in a large skillet over medium heat. Add mushrooms,
onion and garlic; cook for 4 minutes. Add pecans, if using; cook for
one minute. Add remaining ingredients; stir well. Spoon mixture into
a greased 2-quart casserole dish. Cover and bake at 350 degrees for
one hour, or until rice is tender. May be refrigerated or frozen,
unbaked, and baked later as needed. Makes 8 servings.

Dress up steamed vegetables with a quick and yummy cheese
sauce. In a small saucepan, combine one cup evaporated milk
and 1/2 cup shredded cheese of your choice. Stir over
low heat until smooth.

Spare Ribs, Cabbage & Potatoes *Cheryl McIntosh*
Straughn, IN

My mother used to make this dinner for us throughout the winter when we were growing up. I've always made it for my family on New Year's Day and Saint Patrick's Day too. Serve with warm cornbread for a very filling meal.

1-1/2 lbs. pork spare ribs	1 head cabbage, coarsely
6 potatoes, peeled and cut into	chopped
large cubes	salt and pepper to taste

In a large soup pot, cover ribs with water. Bring to a boil over high heat; reduce heat to medium-low. Simmer until meat is very tender and falling off the bone, about 30 minutes. Slice pork off bones and place on a platter to cool; reserve broth in pan. Add potatoes to reserved broth; shred pork and return to pan. Cook over low heat until potatoes are almost tender, 15 minutes. Add cabbage; season with salt and pepper. Simmer for 45 minutes to one hour, or until potatoes and cabbage are tender. Makes 6 servings.

Having friends in to watch the big football game on New Year's Day? Host a tailgate party decked out in your favorite team's colors! Visit a local party supply store for pom-poms, balloons and strings of battery-operated lights. You're sure to score a touchdown!

Italian Sausage & White Beans   *JoAnn*

I love the tradition of eating pork for luck at New Year's, but some of my family & friends don't care for sauerkraut. Everyone likes this dish! I fill up the slow cooker, then we can enjoy watching parades and football together before dinner.

2 12-oz. pkgs. Kielbasa
   sausage, sliced 1/2-inch
   thick
14-1/2 oz. can diced tomatoes
3 15-oz. cans Great Northern
   beans, drained and rinsed
1 c. onion, chopped

1/3 c. bacon, crisply cooked
   and crumbled
1 c. red wine or beef broth
1 t. Italian seasoning
1 t. garlic, minced
1/2 t. pepper
salt to taste

Place sliced sausage in a 5-quart slow cooker. Add tomatoes with juice and remaining ingredients except salt; stir gently. Cover and cook on high setting for 4 to 6 hours. Season with salt at serving time. Serve ladled into soup bowls. Makes 6 to 7 servings.

Love and joy come to you,
And to you your wassail too
And God bless you and send you a Happy New Year,
And God send you a Happy New Year.

–Traditional song

Baked Ham with Mustard-Citrus Dressing

Christina Mamula
Aliquippa, PA

The smell while your ham is baking is mouthwatering!
The bag will help your ham be very moist.

1 T. all-purpose flour
8-lb. fully cooked bone-in
   ham half
1/2 c. mustard

1/2 c. orange marmalade
1/2 t. ground ginger
1/2 t. ground cloves

Add flour to an oven roasting bag; shake to coat inside of bag. Place ham in bag; set aside. Combine remaining ingredients in a small bowl. Coat ham with mustard mixture, using your hands to rub it all over the ham. Close bag; place into a roasting pan. With a knife tip, cut 6 slits in top of bag. Bake at 325 degrees for 2 to 2-1/2 hours, until a meat thermometer reads 140 degrees when inserted in thickest part of ham. Remove from oven; let ham rest for several minutes. Remove to a serving platter and slice. Makes 15 to 20 servings.

Bake up a quiche with leftover holiday ham, chopped veggies and cheese. Put a cup of ingredients in a pie crust, then whisk together 3 eggs and a small can of evaporated milk. Pour into crust and bake at 400 degrees until set, about 20 to 25 minutes. Scrumptious any time of day!

Spiked Sweet Potatoes

Kelli Ritz
Alberta, Canada

My mother always served two kinds of mashed potatoes with our holiday meals. It is a tradition I carried on when making holiday meals for my family. I decided to add a little extra to my sweet potatoes. They are a favorite among family & friends.

3 large or 6 small sweet potatoes
1/4 c. light cream or milk
1/4 c. butter, softened
2 T. maple syrup
1 t. cinnamon
1/4 t. nutmeg

1/4 t. ground ginger
Optional: 1/2 t. salt
2 T. rum, or 2 t. rum extract
1/3 c. toasted candied pecans, finely chopped

Pierce sweet potatoes several times with a fork. Bake at 400 degrees for about 45 minutes, until fork-tender. Let cool; scoop sweet potato pulp into a serving bowl. Add butter, cream, syrup and spices; mash well. Add rum or extract; mix well. Just before serving, sprinkle with pecans. Makes 6 servings.

The year I was in the third grade, I was so excited for Santa to visit. I could not wait for morning to arrive. I went around and changed everyone's watches and clocks, setting them 2 hours ahead. After changing all the clocks, I went around and woke everyone up. Little did they know that instead of 5 a.m., it was only 3 a.m.!

–Sarah Davis, New Bern, NC

Smooth & Creamy Mashed Potatoes

Carol Brownridge
Ontario, Canada

Caesar dressing gives this recipe a special flair. It's a dish that I always make at Christmastime. It's often requested for potlucks too.

8 lbs. baking potatoes, peeled
   and quartered
8-oz. container sour cream
8-oz. pkg. cream cheese,
   softened
1/2 c. milk

2-1/2 c. shredded sharp Cheddar
   cheese, divided
1/4 c. Caesar salad dressing
1/4 c. fresh chives, chopped
salt and pepper to taste

Bring a large pot of salted water to a boil. Add potatoes and cook until fork-tender, about 20 minutes. Drain potatoes; transfer to a large bowl. Mash with a potato masher until potatoes are chunky. Add sour cream, cream cheese, milk and 2 cups Cheddar cheese. Beat potatoes with an electric mixer on medium speed until creamy and smooth; do not overbeat. Stir in salad dressing, chives and seasonings. Transfer to a casserole dish; sprinkle with remaining cheese. Bake at 350 degrees for 30 to 35 minutes, until cheese is melted and bubbly. Makes 8 to 10 servings.

Turn leftover mashed potatoes into twice-baked potatoes. Stir in crumbled bacon, minced onion and shredded cheese to taste and pat into individual ramekins. Bake at 350 degrees for about 30 minutes, until hot and golden...delicious!

Buttery Peas with Lettuce

Diana Chaney
Olathe, KS

*I remember my mother serving garden peas fixed this way at special
meals. It's a simple dish that can be stirred up in a few minutes.*

2 T. butter
14-oz. pkg. frozen baby sweet
    peas, thawed

1 head Bibb lettuce, shredded
1 T. fresh mint, chopped
salt and pepper to taste

Melt butter in a skillet over medium-high heat; add peas and lettuce.
Cook until heated through, about 3 minutes. Stir in mint; season with
salt and pepper. Makes 4 servings.

Snow shovels are a must-have for snowy winters, and they
also make fun welcome signs. Simply give the shovel 2 coats of
chalkboard paint. Once dry, prop it by the door and write cheery
greetings for friends, neighbors, even the letter carrier!

Company Good Sweet Potato Muffins

Sandy Coffey
Cincinnati, OH

You'll get lots of ooh's and ahh's with these scrumptious muffins! Serve them as a special touch for a holiday meal...even serve with coffee for dessert. They're that good!

2-1/2 c. cooked sweet potatoes, mashed
1 c. butter, softened
2 c. sugar
4 eggs, beaten
2-1/2 c. milk
1-1/2 t. lemon extract

7 c. all-purpose flour
2 T. baking powder
1-1/2 t. salt
1-1/2 t. nutmeg
1 t. cinnamon
Garnish: cinnamon-sugar

Stir together warm sweet potatoes, butter and sugar. Add eggs; mix well. Stir in milk and extract; set aside. In a separate bowl, combine remaining ingredients except garnish; add to sweet potato mixture. Stir just until moistened; do not overmix. Spoon batter into paper-lined muffin cups, filling 2/3 full. Top muffins with cinnamon-sugar before baking. Bake at 400 degrees for 25 to 30 minutes. Makes 4 dozen.

Planning a big holiday menu packed with homemade goodness?
Be sure to include items that are easily made ahead. Many
side-dish casseroles, breads and even desserts can be prepared
and frozen as much as one to 2 months in advance,
then thawed overnight and warmed as needed.

Cashew Salad & Poppy Seed Dressing

Barbara Topp
Sparta, NJ

My sister-in-law shared this recipe with me after we visited with them. If you're short on time, you can substitute your favorite bottled poppy seed dressing, but this is easy and good.

1 head iceberg lettuce,
   torn into small pieces
1 c. cashews

1 c. shredded Swiss cheese
1 to 2 T. bacon bits

Combine all ingredients in a large salad bowl; toss to mix. Just before serving, drizzle salad with desired amount of Poppy Seed Dressing; toss again. Makes 8 servings.

Poppy Seed Dressing:

1 c. oil
3/4 c. sugar
1/3 c. white vinegar
1 t. mustard

1 t. poppy seed
1/4 t. dried minced onion
1/8 t. salt

Mix all ingredients in a covered container; shake well. Keep refrigerated. Makes enough for several salads.

Sprinkle a tossed green salad with ruby-red pomegranate seeds for a festive touch.

Christmas Comfort Classics

Mom's Frozen Cranberry Mold

Terri King
Granger, TX

Mom makes this recipe every Christmas. My Aunt Linda in Houston gave it to Mom about 30 years ago and it has been on our family's holiday table every year since.

15-oz. can whole-berry
    cranberry sauce
1 c. crushed pineapple
8-oz. container sour cream
8-oz. pkg cream cheese,
    softened

1/2 c. powdered sugar
2 T. sugar
1 t. vanilla extract
1 c. walnuts or pecans, coarsely
    chopped

In a large bowl, combine cranberry sauce, pineapple with juice and remaining ingredients except nuts. Blend well; stir in chopped nuts. Divide among 12 muffin cups; freeze. To serve, pop out of muffin cups. Makes 12 servings.

Granny's Holiday Pickles

Jenny Bishoff
Mountain Lake, MD

Granny's pickles were present at every holiday, always in beautiful cut-glass relish dishes. As a child, I turned up my nose at them, but as my tastes changed, I realized how delicious they really are!

32-oz. jar dill pickle spears,
    drained
1/2 c. onion, sliced

1 c. sugar
2 T. vinegar

Cut pickles into bite-sized chunks; return to jar. Add onion to jar; top with sugar and vinegar. Add lid; shake gently until sugar dissolves. Refrigerate 24 hours for best flavor. Serves 8 to 10.

When washing cut-glass dishes, add a little white vinegar to the rinse water...the glass will really shine!

Sweets of the Season

Aunt Gail's Sour Cream Sugar Cookies

Lori Roggenbuck
Ubly, MI

This recipe was given to me by my Aunt Gail at my bridal shower back in 1992. I've made these cookies at least a hundred times, so you know they're good! Don't overbake, and these cookies will stay soft until they're all gone.

1 c. butter, softened
1-1/2 c. sugar
3 eggs, beaten
1/2 c. sour cream
1 t. vanilla extract

1 t. baking soda
1/2 t. salt
5 to 6 c. all-purpose flour
Garnish: favorite frosting

In a large bowl, blend butter and sugar until creamy. Stir in eggs, sour cream, vanilla, baking soda and salt. Stir in enough flour to make dough easy to handle. Roll out dough 1/4-inch thick on a floured surface. Cut out dough with cookie cutters. Place on ungreased baking sheets. Bake at 350 degrees for 8 minutes, or until lightly golden. Do not overbake. Decorate with frosting as desired. Makes about 4 dozen.

Here's a simple trick to help cut-out cookies hold their shapes and bake up neatly. Place cookies on a parchment paper-lined baking sheet and pop into the fridge for 10 to 15 minutes, then bake.

Anginetti

Judy Henfey
Cibolo, TX

My mother and aunts would bake for weeks before Christmas. They always gave trays as gifts that were overflowing with their homemade candy and cookies, among them these Italian Christmas cookies. Sweet memories!

1/4 c. butter, softened	2 c. all-purpose flour
1/2 c. sugar	1-1/2 t. baking powder
3 eggs, beaten	Optional: colored sprinkles
1 t. vanilla extract	

In a bowl, blend together butter and sugar; stir in eggs and vanilla. Gradually add flour and baking powder; mix well. Roll dough into 1-1/2 inch balls. Place on ungreased baking sheets, about 2 inches apart. Bake at 350 degrees for 8 to 10 minutes. Cool; spread with Frosting. Decorate with sprinkles, if desired. Makes about 4 dozen.

Frosting:

1-1/2 c. powdered sugar	1-1/2 to 2 t. water
1/2 t. lemon extract	

Mix ingredients together until smooth.

Dig into Mom's or Grandma's recipe box for that extra special treat you remember...and then bake some to share with the whole family.

Cream Cheese Cookies

Becky Kuchenbecker
Ravenna, OH

You will always find these on my cookie trays! I got this recipe many years ago from a co-worker, and it's my most versatile cookie recipe. I have played around with many different cake mixes and extracts. It's a nice soft cookie that can be dropped by a spoon but I prefer to put it thru the cookie press because it is such a soft dough.

1/4 c. butter, softened
8-oz. pkg. cream cheese,
  softened
1 egg, beaten
1 t. almond extract

15-1/4 oz. pkg. yellow cake mix
  with pudding
Optional: 1/2 to 3/4 c.
  all-purpose flour
Garnish: colored sugar

In a large bowl, blend butter and cream cheese. Add egg and extract; mix well. Add dry cake mix; stir well. If dough is very soft, stir in flour, a little at a time, until firmer. Fill a cookie press with dough and press onto ungreased baking sheets, or drop dough by teaspoonfuls onto baking sheets. Sprinkle cookies with colored sugar. Bake at 375 degrees for 8 to 10 minutes, just until cookies start to turn golden. Let stand on baking sheets for a few minutes; remove to a wire rack and finish cooling. Makes about 4 dozen.

Some flavor variations to try:

Chocolate cake mix with almond extract
German chocolate or carrot cake mix with vanilla extract
Lemon cake mix with lemon extract

Check your cupboard for glass tumblers with pretty patterns on the bottom. Just dip the glass in sugar and press to flatten walnut-size balls of dough.

Elf Thumbprints

Jerrilynn Atherton
Biloxi, MS

This is a favorite from my childhood...now transplanted
from Wisconsin to Mississippi!

1 c. butter, room temperature	1 t. vanilla extract
1/2 c. sugar	1/8 t. salt
2 eggs, room temperature,	2 c. all-purpose flour
separated	3/4 c. raspberry jam

Combine butter and sugar in a large bowl. Beat with an electric
mixer on high speed for 3 minutes. Beat in egg yolks and vanilla.
Add flour and salt; mix just until combined. Cover and chill dough
for 30 minutes. Roll dough into one-inch balls. Place on parchment
paper-lined baking sheets. Press each cookie very gently with your
thumb to make a well in the center. Spoon 1/2 teaspoon jam into each
well. Bake at 350 degrees for 12 to 15 minutes, until slightly firm.
Cool on baking sheets for a few minutes; remove to a wire rack and
finish cooling. Makes 2 dozen.

Bubbly Christmas Cheer

Sheri Kohl
Wentzville, MO

Everyone looks forward to this punch. It has become a tradition
that we only serve it during the week of Christmas through
New Year's Day. Let the merriment ensue!

4 c. cranberry juice cocktail	Optional: few drops red food
4 c. pineapple juice	coloring
1/2 c. sugar	2 ltrs. ginger ale, chilled
1 t. almond extract	

In a pitcher, mix together juices, sugar and extract. Add food coloring,
if desired; chill. To serve, fill glasses half-full of juice mixture; top off
with ginger ale. Serves 16.

Buttery Shortbread

Peggy Borrok
Lafayette, LA

I got this recipe years ago from a holiday cookie exchange and have been making them every year since. They taste best the day after making them and for several days after that, so they are perfect for gift-giving. Be sure to use only the best real butter!

1 lb. butter, softened
1-1/4 c. sugar

4-1/2 c. all-purpose flour
Garnish: colored sugar

Combine butter, sugar and flour in a large bowl. With a pastry knife or potato masher, work together ingredients until a crumbly dough forms. Then use your hands to knead dough for about 15 minutes, until dough is sticky with a silky feel. Spray 2, 8"x8" baking pans with non-stick vegetable spray. Divide dough between pans; pat down. With a fork, pierce dough all over to the bottom of pans. Sprinkle with colored sugar. Bake at 325 degrees for 40 to 50 minutes. While still hot, cut each pan of shortbread into 24 squares. Cool completely before removing from pan. Makes 4 dozen.

Dip the edges of cookies in melted chocolate, then roll
in nuts, candy sprinkles or crushed peppermint candies.
Santa will love 'em!

Gingerbread Brownies

Hollie Moots
Marysville, OH

These unusual brownies are the hit of my cookie trays every year!

2-3/4 c. all-purpose flour	1-1/2 c. brown sugar, packed
1 t. baking soda	1/2 c. sugar
1 t. salt	2 eggs plus 1 egg yolk
1 t. cinnamon	1 t. vanilla extract
1 t. ground ginger	1/3 c. molasses
1/4 t. ground cloves	12-oz. pkg. white chocolate
1-1/4 c. butter, softened	chips

In a bowl, whisk together flour, baking soda, salt and spices; set aside. In a separate large bowl, beat butter and sugars until creamy. Stir in eggs and egg yolk, one at a time; add vanilla and molasses. Stir in flour mixture until well mixed. Fold in chocolate chips. Spray a 15"x10" jelly-roll pan with non-stick vegetable spray or line with parchment paper. Spread batter into pan. Bake at 350 degrees for about 25 minutes, until set and golden. Cool completely in pan. Cut into 2-inch bars. Makes 3 dozen.

Molasses is used in many gingerbread recipes. Unless specified, you can use dark molasses for full flavor or light molasses for a milder taste.

Pecan Ozarks

Marian Forck
Chamois, MO

*My Great-Aunt Anna gave this recipe to me. She was
a very special lady and had a heart of gold. She had
many nieces and nephews and was loved by all.*

4 egg whites
1-1/2 c. sugar
1 t. vanilla extract

1-1/2 c. chopped pecans
Optional: 1/2 c. chopped dates

Combine egg whites and sugar in a saucepan. Whisk together over low heat just until warmed. Transfer mixture to a bowl. With an electric mixer on high speed, beat mixture until stiff peaks form. Stir in vanilla; fold in pecans and dates, if desired. Drop by teaspoonfuls onto greased baking sheets. Bake at 325 degrees for 12 minutes. Allow cookies to cool on baking sheets before removing. Makes 5 dozen.

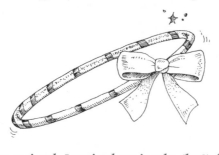

As Christmas Eve arrived, I waited patiently (ha!) for the evening to begin. My sister Lenore and I were allowed to open one small gift that evening. I wanted a hula hoop that Christmas, wanted it bad! Nope, not what I opened. Off to bed we went, until morning. In the middle of the night I heard something. Is it? Could it be? Santa? I heard a hula hoop! I was so excited I ran to tell my sister. "Go back to bed, you don't want to scare him off," she told me. Sadly, I turned back to my room. You really think I was able to sleep after that? I guess I fell off to sleep eventually, because I awoke on Christmas morning recalling all that happened during the night. There it was... my striped hula hoop! I shared my story with the rest of the family with such excitement. "I heard him, I heard him!"

–April Patton, Albuquerque, NM

Grandma's Magical Cookies

Kenn Fuller
Portland, IN

*I can remember going to Grandma's house and the smell of these
delectable cookies would fill her home. Grandma would always
let me cut up the candies...I think I ate more than she used!*

1 c. shortening
2 c. brown sugar, packed
2 eggs, beaten
1/2 c. buttermilk
2 t. baking soda

1 t. salt
3-1/2 c. all-purpose flour
1 c. orange slice candies,
  chopped
1 c. chopped pecans

In a large bowl, combine shortening, brown sugar and eggs; blend
well. Stir in buttermilk, baking soda and salt; gradually mix in flour.
Fold in candies and pecans. Cover and refrigerate for 2 hours. Drop
by heaping teaspoonfuls onto lightly greased baking sheets. Bake at
350 degrees for 8 to 10 minutes. Makes 2 dozen.

Invite friends over for an old-fashioned cookie exchange!
It's a nice break from all the holiday hustle & bustle.
Keep this get-together simple and have friends bring just
a dozen cookies...enough for everyone to sample.

Cherry Twinkles

Kathy Courington
Canton, GA

I still remember my father sitting with the nut grinder chopping the walnuts for these cookies. We knew then it was time for Cherry Twinkles! My grown granddaughter today still requests these cookies every holiday season.

2/3 c. shortening
1/2 c. sugar
2 eggs, separated
2 T. orange zest
2 T. lemon zest

2 t. lemon juice
2 c. all-purpose flour
1-1/2 to 2 c. chopped walnuts
10-oz. jar maraschino cherries,
    well drained and halved

Line baking sheets with parchment paper or lightly spray baking sheets with non-stick vegetable spray; set aside. Combine shortening, sugar, beaten egg yolks, zests and juice; blend well. Gradually stir in flour. Form dough into balls by teaspoonfuls. Dip balls into lightly beaten egg whites; roll in chopped walnuts. Place balls on baking sheets; press a cherry half into the center of each ball. Bake at 350 degrees for about 15 minutes, just until set and lightly golden. Cool completely. Makes 3 dozen.

Christmas Day is a day of joy and charity.
May God make you very rich in both.

–Phillips Brooks

Borecky Pudding Cookies

Judy Borecky
Escondido, CA

These cookies are easy to make. Back in the early 1960s, I made them for our sons all the time. You can change the flavor of the pudding to make cookies in colors for any holiday.

1 c. butter, softened
2 eggs
2 3-oz. pkgs. instant pudding
    mix (coconut, chocolate,
    lemon, pistachio or
    butterscotch)
1/4 c. sugar
1 t. vanilla extract
2 c. all-purpose flour

1 t. baking soda
1 t. cream of tartar
1/4 t. salt
1/2 c. chopped walnuts
    or pecans
Optional: 1/2 c. sweetened
    flaked coconut
Optional: jelly beans

In a bowl, combine butter, eggs, dry pudding mix, sugar, vanilla, flour, baking soda, cream of tartar and salt. Beat with an electric mixer on medium speed, just until blended. Stir in nuts and coconut, if using. Drop dough onto ungreased baking sheets, 2 tablespoons per cookie. Bake at 350 degrees for 14 minutes, or until lightly golden. Cool completely; decorate with Vanilla Glaze. May top cookies with a colored jelly bean, for example, white jelly beans for coconut cookies. Makes 3-1/2 dozen.

Vanilla Glaze:

1/4 c. butter, sliced
3 T. half-and-half
1/8 t. salt

2 c. powdered sugar
1 t. vanilla extract

Heat butter with half-and-half; remove from heat. Add remaining ingredients; whisk until smooth. Let stand for about 10 minutes; drizzle or spoon over cookies.

Chill December brings the sleet,
Blazing fire, and Christmas treat.

–Sara Coleridge

Nut-Filled Cookies

Patti Bogetti
Magnolia, DE

*This is just one of my favorite cookies that our mom would make
every year from her big collection of Christmas cookie recipes.*

1 lb. cottage cheese
1 lb. butter, softened

4 c. all-purpose flour

In a large bowl, combine cottage cheese, butter and flour. Beat with an
electric mixer on medium speed, using a paddle attachment, until well
blended. Wrap dough in plastic wrap and refrigerate overnight. At
baking time, roll out dough thinly on a lightly floured surface. Cut into
2-inch squares. Spoon one to 2 teaspoons Nut Filling into the center
of each square. Overlap 2 opposite corners of each square, pinching
lightly. Place on ungreased baking sheets. Bake at 375 degrees for
30 minutes; cool. Makes 4 dozen.

Nut Filling:

2 c. ground walnuts
1-1/2 c. brown sugar, packed
6 T. all-purpose flour
4 t. cinnamon

6 T. butter, melted
4 to 6 T. milk, warmed
    and cooled

Combine all ingredients and mix well, adding milk until mixture
is moistened.

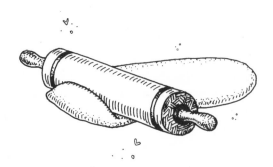

Sprinkle powdered sugar on the countertop when rolling out cookie
dough...so much tastier than using flour and it works just as well!

Granny's Swedish Heirloom Cookies

Melissa Palmer
DeLand, FL

One of my family's favorite Christmas traditions was going to Granny Buettner's little house to pick up her tasty cookies! As with any fond memory, it isn't Christmas for us until we make Granny's delicious cookies. Enjoy!

1 c. butter, softened	1-1/4 c. ground pecans
2 c. powdered sugar, divided	or almonds
1/2 t. salt	1 T. water
2 c. all-purpose flour	1 T. vanilla extract

In a bowl, blend butter, one cup powdered sugar and salt; gradually stir in flour. Add nuts, water and vanilla; mix well. Shape dough by tablespoonfuls into crescents; place on ungreased baking sheets. May also shape into balls; flatten with a fork dipped in water. Place an oven rack in the center of oven. Bake, one sheet at a time, at 325 degrees for about 20 minutes, until cookies are golden on the bottom. While cookies are still warm, drop them into a bowl filled with remaining powdered sugar. Shake bowl until cookies are covered completely. Cool; shake cookies again in powdered sugar. Makes 2 dozen.

A muffin tin makes a handy container when you're decorating with lots of different candy sprinkles and colored sugars. Just fill each cup with a different garnish.

Cherry-Walnut Bars

Violet Leonard
Chesapeake, VA

These bars are decadent and rich. Not a typical Christmas cookie, but something my mom and Grandma made each year at Christmas time. We grew up on a small farm and my mother was a fantastic cook. As a mother of 12 kids, eight of them boys, she had to be! Sweets were always available in our house. This was one of her favorites. A little goes a long way, these are very sweet.

2-1/4 c. all-purpose flour
1/2 c. sugar
1 c. butter, softened
2 eggs plus 1 egg yolk, beaten
1-1/2 c. brown sugar, packed
1/2 t. baking powder

1/2 t. salt
1/2 c. maraschino cherries, chopped
1/2 c. chopped walnuts
2 c. powdered sugar

Combine flour, sugar and butter in a bowl; mix until mixture resembles coarse crumbs. Press into the bottom of an ungreased 13"x9" baking pan. Bake at 350 degrees for 15 minutes; cool. In a separate bowl, combine remaining ingredients except powdered sugar; spread over baked crust. Bake at 350 degrees for 20 minutes. Remove from oven. Cool; spread with Frosting. Cut into small squares. Store tightly covered in the refrigerator. Makes 2 dozen.

Frosting:

1 egg white, beaten
2 T. butter, melted

2 T. maraschino cherry juice
2 c. powdered sugar

Combine all ingredients; beat until smooth.

If a recipe calls for softened butter, grate chilled sticks with a cheese grater. The butter will soften in just minutes.

Grandmother's Spitzbuben

Pearl Teiserskas
Brookfield, IL

If I had a time machine, I know exactly where I'd go...back to my German-speaking, gray-haired, wire-rimmed spectacles-wearing, full-figured Great-Grandma's kitchen. A couple weeks before Christmas, Grandma always got into her baking mode. You could smell the cookies baking as you pulled into the drive. These are oversized raspberry jam sandwich cookies.

1/2 c. butter, softened	2-1/4 c. all-purpose flour
2/3 c. sugar	1/4 t. salt
1 egg, beaten	2/3 c. raspberry preserves
1/4 t. vanilla extract	Garnish: powdered sugar

Combine butter and sugar in a bowl. With an electric mixer on medium speed, beat until light and fluffy. Beat in egg and vanilla; set aside. In a separate bowl, mix flour and salt; stir into butter mixture until combined. Roll out dough on a lightly floured surface, 1/4-inch thick. Using a 3-inch round cookie cutter, cut out 18 rounds, re-rolling dough as necessary. Using a one-inch round cookie cutter, cut the centers out of 9 rounds; discard centers. Place all dough rounds on parchment paper-lined baking sheets. Bake at 375 degrees for about 10 minutes, until lightly golden. Let cookies cool on a wire rack. Spread 9 solid rounds with one tablespoon preserves each; top with a cut-out round. Dust lightly with powdered sugar. Makes 9 large cookies.

Tuck a cookie into a cellophane bag and add a tag stamped, "Thanks for all you do!" Make up a batch to hand out to the mail carrier, the babysitter, the bus driver and all those other helpful folks we just don't remember to thank as often as we might.

Old-Fashioned Peanut Butter Cookies

Diana Krol
Nickerson, KS

My Grandma Hersh had a brown crock cookie jar that was almost always filled with peanut butter cookies. I suspect they were her favorite! This recipe makes soft, chewy cookies...delicious!

2-1/2 c. all-purpose flour
1 t. baking powder
1 t. baking soda
1/4 t. salt
1 c. butter, melted

1 c. creamy peanut butter
1 c. sugar
1 c. brown sugar, packed
2 eggs, beaten
1 t. vanilla extract

In a bowl, combine flour, baking powder, baking soda and salt; mix well and set aside. In a large bowl, beat butter and peanut butter until smooth. Mix in sugars; stir in eggs and vanilla. Blend in flour mixture, mixing well. If dough is very soft, cover and chill until firm. Shape dough into one-inch balls. Place 2 inches apart on ungreased baking sheets; flatten slightly with a fork dipped in sugar. Bake at 350 degrees for 9 minutes. Makes 6 dozen.

Campfires, toasted marshmallows and ghost stories are
a classic combination. Why not whip up a batch of s'mores
to snack on and gather the family by the fireplace for
a reading of "A Christmas Carol"?

Sweets *of* the Season

Mission Crybabies

Nancy Osborn
Ontario, Canada

My mother-in-law gave me this recipe for a soft molasses cookie...it's the only cookie her son would eat! It is a very old recipe. I make these cookies every year for him.

2 c. raisins
1 t. baking soda
1 c. strong hot coffee
1 c. shortening, or 1/2 c.
　　shortening plus 1/2 c. butter
1 c. sugar
2 eggs, beaten

1/2 c. molasses
1 T. vinegar
4 c. all-purpose flour
2 t. cinnamon
1 t. ground ginger
1/2 t. salt

Place raisins in a bowl. Sprinkle with baking soda; pour hot coffee over raisins. Set aside. Meanwhile, in a separate large bowl, combine shortening and sugar; beat until light. Add eggs; beat until pale and light. Beat in molasses and vinegar; stir in raisin mixture. In another bowl, combine flour, salt and spices; mix well and add to shortening mixture. Beat very well until a thin dough forms. Spoon dough by mounded teaspoonfuls onto buttered baking sheets, about 1-1/4 inches apart. Bake at 375 degrees for 7 to 9 minutes; do not overbake. Cool on a wire rack. Makes 5 dozen.

The best gift busy parents could receive...an offer to babysit for an afternoon or an evening. While they're out holiday shopping, entertain the kids with a simple activity like baking cookies or making sweet handprint cards for Mom & Dad. Your gesture is sure to be appreciated.

Kathy's Buttermilk Brownies

Kathy Vatthauer
Red Lake Falls, MN

For more than 30 years, I have baked these brownies at least twice a month and they continue to be a favorite. My husband and his relatives who all farm together enjoy these during coffee breaks. They always let me know when the brownie plate is empty!

2 c. sugar	1 t. vanilla extract
2 c. all-purpose flour	1 c. butter, sliced
1 t. baking soda	1/4 c. baking cocoa
1/2 c. buttermilk	1 c. water
2 eggs, beaten	

Mix together sugar, flour and baking soda in a large bowl. Add buttermilk, eggs and vanilla; stir well and set aside. In a saucepan over medium-low heat, melt butter with cocoa. Add water; bring mixture to a boil. Fold butter mixture into sugar mixture; stir until well mixed. Pour batter into a greased 15"x10" jelly-roll pan. Bake at 350 degrees for 20 minutes. Pour hot Frosting over brownies. Cut into squares. Makes 2-1/2 dozen.

Frosting:

1 c. brown sugar, packed	1/2 c. semi-sweet chocolate
3 T. butter, sliced	chips
3 T. milk	

Combine brown sugar, butter and milk in a saucepan over medium heat. Cook, stirring constantly, until brown sugar dissolves and mixture almost reaches a boil; do not boil. Remove from heat; add chocolate chips. Stir until melted and smooth.

Give brownies and bar cookies a fresh new look. Instead of bars or squares, cut cookies into diamond shapes.

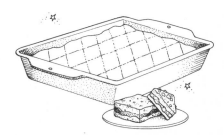

Sweets of the Season

Soft Sugared Gingerbread

Judy Henfey
Cibolo, TX

A great cake to make on a cold winter's day! It's very easy and makes your home smell wonderful when it is baking. Serve with a piping-hot cup of coffee. Enjoy!

1 c. margarine
2-1/4 c. sugar, divided
2 eggs, beaten
1 t. baking soda
1 c. milk, room temperature

3 c. all-purpose flour
1 t. salt
1 t. ground ginger
1 t. cinnamon
Optional: whipped cream

In a large bowl, blend margarine and 2 cups sugar; stir in eggs. Dissolve baking soda in milk; add to margarine mixture. In a separate bowl, combine flour, salt and ginger. Slowly add to margarine mixture. Pour batter into a greased 13"x9" baking pan. Bake at 325 degrees for 40 minutes. Combine remaining sugar and cinnamon; sprinkle over cake. Cut into squares. If desired, top with whipped cream. Makes 10 to 12 servings.

Red Velvet Poke Cake

Jenny Bishoff
Mountain Lake Park, MD

My mom told me about this recipe and I just had to try it! It's a new way to indulge in an old favorite.

15-1/4 oz. pkg. red velvet
  cake mix
2 3.4-oz. pkgs. instant
  cheesecake pudding mix

4 c. milk
Garnish: whipped topping

Bake cake according to package directions, using a 13"x9" baking pan. While cake is still warm, poke large holes with the end of a wooden spoon; set aside. In a bowl, whisk pudding mix with milk for 2 minutes. Pour pudding over cake, filling the holes. Cover and refrigerate 2 hours to overnight. Cut into squares; top with whipped topping. Makes 12 to 16 servings.

Grandma's Butter Cookies

Anett Yeager
Battle Ground, WA

*Grandma would make these cookies for all the grandkids
on Christmas Eve. It was our tradition to eat them
after we opened our presents.*

1 c. butter, room temperature
1/2 c. sugar
2 c. all-purpose flour

1 egg white
1 t. water
Optional: colored sprinkles

In a large bowl, combine butter and sugar; stir until creamy. Slowly stir in flour; form dough into a ball. If too soft, add a little more flour. On a floured surface, roll out dough to about 1/4-inch thick. Cut out with cookie cutters; place on ungreased baking sheets. In a small bowl, beat egg white with water; brush over cookies. Add sprinkles, if desired. Bake at 350 degrees for 6 to 7 minutes, until golden. Cool on a wire rack. Makes 2 dozen.

My Bubbie (grandmother) was the best cook and baker in the world. No one has her recipes, but I can still taste everything she ever made. Her muffins called Mexican Hats, because that's what they looked like. Her Mun Cookies with poppy seeds called pletzele. Nothing compares...always shaped as perfect spades, hearts, clubs and aces. I made so many versions from different cookbooks, but they didn't taste like hers. Then I found someone on the internet from New York City who had shared a recipe for Mun Cookies on her food blog. I made them again. They tasted very very close to hers! I ended up making them in guitar shapes. I dipped them in tea with milk, just as Bubbie did it for me. Sitting there and eating these new Mun Cookies, I closed my eyes and Bubbie was there with me all over again.

–Linda Saslove, Ontario, Canada

Grandma's Jelly Cookies

Pam McCourt
Marlboro, NC

This simple recipe has been used in our family for four generations. I'm happy to have it in my grandmother's handwriting. My mother made these cookies often, so they bring back memories of my childhood. We used to enjoy them for dessert, warm from the oven. They are easy to put together

1 c. shortening
1 c. sugar
2 eggs, beaten

1 t. vanilla extract
2-3/4 c. all-purpose flour
1/4 c. favorite jelly or jam

In a large bowl, mix together shortening, sugar, eggs and vanilla. Stir in flour. Roll into one-inch balls; place on ungreased baking sheets. Using your thumb, press an indent gently in the middle of each cookie. Fill with 1/2 teaspoon jelly or jam. Bake at 375 degrees for 10 to 15 minutes, until golden on the edges. Makes 2 dozen.

Jams and preserves keep well, so pick up a few jars of local specialties like beach plum, peach or boysenberry on family trips. Later, use them to bake up thumbprint cookies or jam bars. The flavors are sure to bring back happy memories!

Cranberry Cookies

Glenda Tolbert
Moore, SC

I fell in love with this cookie when I first encountered it at a church tea party. No detail was spared...a historic home was rented, everyone brought their own tea cups and favorite cookies. The only oversight...the hostesses forgot to boil water for our tea! It didn't take long before the situation was remedied and we were sampling different flavors of tea. Since then, I serve this cookie at the holidays. My relatives insist on it!

1 c. butter, softened
1 c. brown sugar, packed
1/3 c. sugar
2 eggs, beaten
1 t. vanilla extract
2 t. orange flavoring oil
1-1/2 c. all-purpose flour
1 t. baking soda

1/2 t. salt
3 c. quick-cooking oats, uncooked
1 c. white chocolate chips
1 c. chopped walnuts
6-oz. pkg. sweetened dried cranberries

In a large bowl, blend butter and sugars. Add eggs, vanilla and orange oil; mix well. In a separate bowl, mix flour, baking soda and salt; add to butter mixture and stir well. Fold in remaining ingredients. Drop dough by rounded tablespoonfuls onto greased baking sheets. Bake at 350 degrees for 15 minutes, until edges are golden; check at 12 minutes. Makes about 3 dozen.

Nestle cookies in paper cupcake liners and arrange them
in a shallow box or tray for a pretty buffet table presentation.

Apple-Cranberry Bake

Angela Bissette
Middlesex, NC

This is a recipe that my mother makes during the holidays.
It is delicious served with ice cream or with a hot cup
of coffee on a cold winter evening.

4 c. Granny Smith or Fuji apples,
  peeled, cored and diced
2 c. fresh cranberries
2 t. lemon juice
1 c. sugar
1 c. chopped pecans

1-1/3 c. quick-cooking oats,
  uncooked
1/3 c. brown sugar, packed
1/2 c. butter, melted
Optional: vanilla ice cream

Layer apples and cranberries in a greased 2-quart casserole dish. Sprinkle with lemon juice and sugar. Combine remaining ingredients in a bowl; stir until mixture is crumbly. Sprinkle over fruit. Bake, uncovered, at 350 degrees for one hour. Serve warm, topped with ice cream if desired. Serves 8 to 10.

Be sure to pick up a pint or two of ice cream in cinnamon, peppermint and other delicious seasonal flavors when they're available. What a special touch for holiday desserts!

Jack Horner Plum Pie

Janis Parr
Ontario, Canada

This pie was one of my mom's favorite desserts. I remember coming home from school and smelling this pie baking before I even opened the door. After looking for the recipe for four years, I finally found it! I just have to share it it with you.

2 9-inch pie crusts, unbaked
2 14-oz. cans plums, drained
   and syrup reserved
2-1/2 T. cornstarch
1/4 t. cinnamon

1/4 t. nutmeg
2 t. butter
1 T. lemon juice
Garnish: vanilla ice cream

Place one pie crust in a 9" pie plate; set aside. Remove any pits from plums; cut plums into quarters and set aside. In a saucepan over medium-low heat, combine cornstarch and spices with a little of the reserved plum syrup; stir together. Add remaining syrup; bring to a boil. Cook and stir for about 3 minutes, until mixture thickens. Remove from heat; stir in butter, lemon juice and plums. Cool slightly; pour into unbaked pie crust. Cover with remaining crust; press edges of crust to seal and cut several vents with a knife tip. Bake at 425 degrees for 12 minutes. Reduce heat to 350 degrees; continue baking for 25 minutes more, or until crust is lightly golden. Cool; serve with a scoop of vanilla ice cream. Serves 8.

Instead of an elaborate holiday party, host a dessert open house for friends and neighbors. Serve lots of cookies with coffee, tea and festive mulled cider or hot cocoa. Just add fun and fellowship for a delightful no-stress afternoon!

Peach & Apricot Pie

Marlene Burns
Swisher, IA

My mom liked to make this yummy pie for the holidays.

2 6-oz. pkgs. dried apricots, halved
2 T. orange liqueur or orange juice
2 T. water
3/4 t. cinnamon, divided

1 c. plus 1 T. sugar, divided
5 T. cornstarch
3 16-oz. pkgs. frozen sliced peaches, thawed
11-oz. pkg. pie crust mix
1 egg, beaten

In a microwave-safe bowl, combine apricots, orange liqueur or juice and water. Cover; microwave on high in one-minute intervals until apricots soften. Uncover and cool. In a separate large bowl, stir together one cup sugar, cornstarch and 1/2 teaspoon cinnamon until blended; stir in apricot mixture and peaches. Set aside. Prepare crust mix as package directs for a 2-crust pie, adding remaining cinnamon. Line a 9" pie plate with one crust; spoon fruit mixture into crust. Cut remaining crust into strips; arrange on pie to make a lattice-top crust. Brush crust with beaten egg; sprinkle with remaining sugar. Set pie plate on a baking sheet on rack in center of oven. Bake at 375 degrees for one hour and 25 minutes, until bubbly and crust is golden. Makes 8 servings.

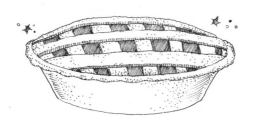

A woven lattice pie crust is impressive, but there's an easier way to make a lattice! Cut pie crust into one-inch wide strips. Place half of the strips across the pie filling in one direction, then place the remaining strips at right angles. Bake as usual.

Christmas Rum Cake

Doreen Adams-Minasian
Citrus Heights, CA

This cake has been a tradition in our family for many years. Originally it was served for our Christmas Eve dessert, but after a sumptuous buffet on Christmas Eve, nobody had room for cake! So everyone took a piece home and ate it on Christmas morning while opening the gifts that Santa had brought. It is our favorite Christmas recipe, enjoyed year after year.

1/3 c. chopped nuts
15-1/4 oz. pkg. yellow cake mix
3-oz. pkg. instant vanilla
   pudding mix
1/2 c. cold water
1/2 c. rum
4 eggs, beaten
1/2 c. oil

Grease and flour a Bundt® pan. Sprinkle nuts into bottom of pan; set aside. Combine dry cake mix, dry pudding mix and remaining ingredients; beat well. Pour batter over nuts. Bake at 325 degrees for one hour. Cool; place a serving plate on top of pan and turn cake out onto plate. Pierce top of cake all over with a fork; drizzle with Glaze. Makes 8 to 10 servings.

Glaze:

1/4 c. butter
1/2 c. sugar
2 T. water
1/4 c. rum

Melt butter in a saucepan. Stir in water and sugar. Boil for 5 minutes, stirring constantly. Remove from heat; stir in rum.

Turn a Bundt® cake into a holiday wreath. Drizzle with frosting, then sprinkle chopped green and red candied cherries over the top. Twist a long strip of red fruit leather into a jaunty bow to complete the wreath...simple!

Sweets of the Season

Great-Grandmother's Apple Pan Dowdy

Bev Weeks
New Brunswick, Canada

My great-grandmother used to make this very old recipe as a very special treat in the wintertime, using dried apples from her and Great-Grandfather's orchard, maple syrup from their trees, cream from their cows and butter churned in her kitchen. It was so good and made everyone feel so special!

6 McIntosh or Cortland apples,
   peeled, cored and sliced
1/2 c. brown sugar, packed
1/2 t. cinnamon
1/4 t. ground nutmeg
3/4 c. maple syrup
3 T. water

4 T. butter, melted and divided
1-1/4 c. all-purpose flour
1/4 t. salt
1/3 c. butter, softened
3 T. milk
Garnish: whipped cream or
   ice cream, maple syrup

In an ungreased 2-quart casserole dish, mix apples, brown sugar and spices; set aside. In a bowl, combine maple syrup, water and 2 tablespoons melted butter. Pour over apple mixture; set aside. In a separate bowl, combine flour, salt and softened butter; mix with a pastry blender or your hands. Sprinkle with milk, one tablespoon at a time; stir until flour mixture is moistened. Gather dough into a ball; shape and flatten. Roll out dough on a floured surface to fit casserole dish; place dough over apple mixture. Brush with remaining melted butter. Bake at 350 degrees for 30 minutes. Remove from oven. With a sharp knife, cut or break crust into small pieces; mix with apples. Return to oven and bake for an additional 20 to 25 minutes. Serve warm, topped with whipped cream or ice cream; drizzle each serving with a small amount of maple syrup. Makes 8 servings.

Warm caramel topping makes a delightful drizzle over baked apple desserts. Just heat it in the microwave for a few seconds.

White Chocolate Bread Pudding

Debbie Thurmond
Shreveport, LA

This is one of my husband's favorites. I've made it for his birthday, and it is great for potlucks and entertaining as well. I have also used milk chocolate and semi-sweet chocolate for this recipe. Yum!

1 loaf French or Italian bread,
   cut into small cubes
4 eggs
4 c. whipping cream
2 c. sugar

2 t. vanilla extract
Optional: 3/4 to 1 c. chopped
   pecans
cinnamon to taste
1/2 c. butter, melted

Place bread cubes in a large bowl. Cover loosely and let stand for several hours to overnight to dry out. In a separate bowl, beat eggs; beat in cream, sugar and vanilla. Pour over bread cubes; toss to coat. Fold in pecans, if using. Let stand for 10 minutes so bread can absorb egg mixture. Spoon into a 13"x9" baking pan sprayed with non-stick vegetable spray. Press down lightly with spoon; sprinkle with cinnamon. Drizzle melted butter evenly over pudding. Bake, uncovered, at 350 degrees for 45 to 55 minutes. Remove from oven. While pudding cools, make White Chocolate Sauce. (Do not make sauce until pudding is done, as it will be too hard to pour.) Pour sauce over pudding; serve warm. Makes 10 to 12 servings.

White Chocolate Sauce:

3/4 c. butter, sliced
6-oz. pkg. white baking
   chocolate, broken up

1 c. powdered sugar
4 to 6 t. water

Place butter and chocolate in a microwave-safe bowl. Microwave for 30 seconds at a time, stirring after each, until completely melted. Add powdered sugar, a little at a time; whisk to blend together well. Stir in water, a tiny bit at a time, until sauce is smooth, creamy and easy to pour.

Mom's Famous Pecan Crispies

Sue Klapper
Muskego, WI

Once you've tried my mom's pecan cookies, you will
never buy store-bought again...I promise!

1/2 c. shortening
1/2 c. butter, softened
2-1/2 c. light brown sugar,
   packed
2 eggs, beaten

2-1/2 c. all-purpose flour
1/2 t. baking soda
1/4 t. salt
1 t. vanilla extract
1 c. chopped pecans

In a large bowl, blend shortening, butter and brown sugar. Add eggs; beat well and set aside. In a separate bowl, combine flour, baking soda and salt. Mix well and add to shortening mixture; stir well. Stir in vanilla and pecans. Drop dough by teaspoonfuls onto greased baking sheets, 2 inches apart. Bake at 350 degrees for 12 to 15 minutes. Makes 2 dozen.

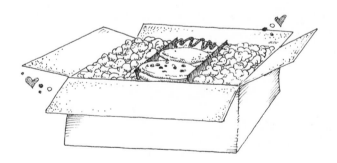

Mailing cookies is a snap...just follow these pointers. Choose firm cookies such as sliced, drop or bar cookies; avoid frosted or filled ones. Line a sturdy box with plastic bubble wrap (or plain popcorn!) and pack cookies in a single layer with wax paper between the layers.

Grandma's Chocolate Fudge

Jacklyn Buckler
Shelby, OH

I loved to make candy with my grandma at Christmastime. I can still see Grandma by her old-fashioned stove, stirring chocolate fudge or potato candy with love for all of my five brothers & sisters to enjoy, every Christmas down home.

2-1/4 c. sugar
2 T. butter, sliced
3/4 c. evaporated milk
1/4 t. salt
16 marshmallows

1 c. semi-sweet chocolate chips
1 t. vanilla extract
Optional: chopped nuts or
    candied cherries

In a large saucepan over medium heat, combine sugar, butter, evaporated milk, salt and marshmallows. Bring to a full rolling boil. Boil, stirring constantly, for 5 minutes. Remove from heat; add remaining ingredients. Stir until chocolate is melted and smooth. Pour into a greased 9"x5" loaf pan; cool completely. Cut into small squares. Makes 18 pieces.

A cold, sunny winter day is perfect weather for making fudge
and other candies. Don't try to make candy on a rainy
or humid day, as it may not set up properly.

3-Ingredient Christmas Bark

*Stephanie Turner
Meridian, ID*

*Kids love helping to make this festive treat. No one
will know it took only five minutes to make!*

1 lb. white melting chocolate
15 chocolate sandwich cookies,
   broken up into large chunks

6 to 8 peppermint candy canes,
   broken into small pieces

Melt chocolate in a double boiler or a microwave; stir until smooth.
Pour chocolate onto a wax paper-lined baking sheet. Spread evenly
over baking sheet with a spatula. Quickly arrange cookie and candy
pieces over melted chocolate. With a piece of wax paper, gently
press toppings into chocolate. Refrigerate on baking sheet for about
30 minutes, until set and firm. Break into pieces. Store loosely covered.
Makes 20 servings.

Start a simple holiday scrapbook to update every year with
the family's Christmas card, gift wrap samples, copies of letters
to Santa, notes from special guests and of course holiday
snapshots...such fun to look at year after year!

Peanut Butter Balls

Kathleen Elverston
Federal Way, WA

This is a recipe my mom has been making for most holidays and special occasions I can remember. It is so good you can't stop at having only one piece! I use a nut grinder to make the crumbs.

2 c. graham crackers, finely
   crushed
16-oz. pkg. powdered sugar
1 c. margarine, room
   temperature

3/4 c. creamy peanut butter
1 c. sweetened flaked coconut
1 c. ground walnuts
1 t. vanilla extract

Combine all ingredients in a large bowl. Mix well; form into one-inch balls. Set balls on a wax paper-lined baking sheet; refrigerate until firm. Using a toothpick, dip each ball into Chocolate Coating, covering well. Return balls to baking sheet; refrigerate until coating has hardened. Store in a sealed container in the refrigerator. Makes 2 to 3 dozen.

Chocolate Coating:

2 12-oz. pkgs. semi-sweet
   chocolate chips

1/2 bar paraffin, chopped

Combine ingredients in a double boiler; melt and stir until smooth.

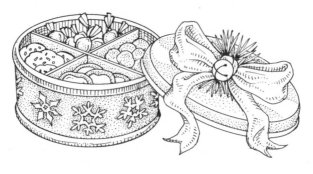

Give a cookie sampler! Just use poster board to divide a round tin into equal sections. Fill each with a different cookie or candy. Sure to be appreciated!

Cranberry-Walnut Fudge

*Judy Lange
Imperial, PA*

Christmas Fudge is what we call this...pretty to look at, delicious to eat! Back in the good old days and many moons ago my mother always made chocolate fudge for Christmas. She would put the finished pan on the floor in front of the back door to cool. My brother Danny came running into the kitchen and accidentally stepped in the fudge. His little footprint was on top! That Christmas, our fudge was made with a footprint of love.

3-oz. pkg. cream cheese,
   softened
1/2 c. creamy vanilla frosting
1/2 c. powdered sugar
12-oz. pkg. white chocolate
   chips

1 t. orange zest
1/4 c. chopped walnuts
3/4 c. sweetened dried
   cranberries

Line a 9"x9" baking pan with aluminum foil, extending foil over sides for easy removal. Spray pan with non-stick vegetable spray; set aside. In a bowl, combine cream cheese, frosting and powdered sugar; blend well and set aside. Melt chocolate chips in a small saucepan over low heat; stir until smooth. Stir melted chocolate into cream cheese mixture; stir in orange zest, walnuts and cranberries. Spread in foil-lined pan. Cover and refrigerate for about one hour, until firm. Cut into squares. Makes 2 dozen.

For an easy sweet & salty treat, pop your favorite
microwave popcorn, spread out on a wax paper-lined baking
sheet, and drizzle with melted white chocolate. Let harden,
then pack into airtight containers. Scrumptious!

Blizzard Party Mix

Elizabeth McCord
Bartlett, TN

This is a kid-pleaser, and adults love it too! It's great for parties, tailgating or movie night. Make it festive with red & green candy-coated chocolates. Make a big batch and keep it on hand!

5 c. bite-size crispy corn or
   rice cereal squares, or a
   mixture of both
4 c. doughnut-shaped oat cereal
2 c. pretzel sticks, coarsely
   broken

2 c. dry-roasted peanuts
12-oz. pkg. plain or peanut
   butter candy-coated
   chocolates
24-oz. pkg. white melting
   chocolate, broken up

Combine all ingredients except melting chocolate in a large bowl; toss to mix and set aside. Melt chocolate in a double boiler or a microwave; stir until smooth. Slowly pour melted chocolate over cereal mixture; stir to coat evenly. Spread mixture on a wax or parchment paper-lined baking sheet. Cool; break apart and store in an airtight container or large plastic zipping bag. Makes 16 servings.

For fun little gifts, fill clear plastic cups with a crunchy snack mix. Wrap in colorful cellophane and heap the cups in a basket. Visitors can choose a favorite to take home.

Pineapple-Coconut Snowballs

Charlotte Smith
Alexandria, PA

I make these little treats every Christmas for my cookie exchange and also for my cookie table that I set up when company comes. They sure don't last long! This is a nice item to give as a gift...place in cute mini cupcake liners and set in small boxes.

8-oz. pkg. cream cheese,
   softened
8-oz. can crushed pineapple,
   very well drained

2-1/2 c. sweetened flaked
   coconut

In a small bowl, beat cream cheese and pineapple until blended. Cover and refrigerate for 20 minutes. Form into one-inch balls; roll in coconut to coat. Place on a wax paper-lined baking sheet. Refrigerate for 6 hours, or until firm. Makes 2 dozen.

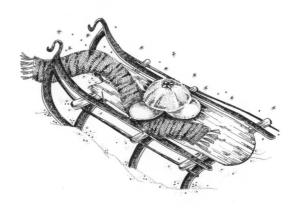

One Christmas break, we were fortunate enough to have several inches of snow. We grabbed our sleds and headed to a state park not too far from our house. We were having a good time sledding, when Dad decided he was going to show us how it was really done. He grabbed the sled and headed over to a steep hill. Dad sat on the sled and as he was picking up speed, he suddenly dropped onto a set of stairs concealed by the snow. We couldn't contain our laughter as he bounced down the stairs!

–Jenny Devening, Freetown, IN

Holiday Trifle Cups

Eleanor Dionne
Beverly, MA

*This dessert used to be one of my favorites about 35 years ago,
I would make it a lot. Everyone enjoyed these.*

1-1/2 c. pound cake, cubed
2 T. orange juice
3 T. raspberry preserves
1 T. water
3-oz. pkg. instant vanilla
    pudding mix

1-1/2 c. cold milk
1-1/2 c. frozen whipped topping,
    thawed and divided
Garnish: maraschino cherries

Divide cake cubes among 6 dessert glasses; sprinkle with orange juice.
Combine preserves and water in a cup; spoon over cake cubes and
set aside. In a bowl, whisk pudding mix with milk for 2 minutes; blend
in one cup whipped topping. Spoon pudding mixture into glasses.
Garnish with remaining topping; top each with a maraschino cherry.
Makes 6 servings.

If the kids just can't wait 'til Christmas, celebrate early on
Saint Nicholas Day, December 6th! Each child sets out their shoes
the night before...Saint Nick will fill the shoes of those who've
behaved with treats and small presents.

Cranberry Mousse

Cheryl Westfall
Surprise, AZ

A requested recipe by family members for all holiday gatherings!

1 c. cranberry juice cocktail
3-oz. pkg. raspberry gelatin mix
15-oz. can whole-berry
    cranberry sauce

1 c. heavy cream, whipped
Optional: additional whipped
    cream

In a saucepan over medium heat, heat cranberry juice to boiling. Add gelatin mix; stir until dissolved. Remove from heat; stir in cranberry sauce. Cover and chill until mixture is thickened. In a bowl, beat cream with an electric mixer on high speed until soft peaks form. Fold whipped cream into gelatin mixture; spoon into a glass bowl or individual dessert dishes. Cover and chill until firm. Garnish with additional whipped cream, if desired. Serves 8.

Real whipped cream makes any dessert extra special. It's easy too. In a chilled bowl, combine one cup whipping cream with 1/4 cup powdered sugar and one teaspoon vanilla extract. Beat with chilled beaters until stiff peaks form.

Coconut Eggnog

Fara Baker
Tuscola, TX

I first made this for a Christmas cookie exchange for my military family. Everyone loved it so much that as soon as the fall season arrived, I was required to make it for every gathering we had. I don't think I made anything else for potlucks from September through February for five years! If you don't have a double boiler, a heavy-bottomed saucepan over low heat would work.

2 egg yolks, beaten
12-oz. can evaporated milk
14-oz. can sweetened condensed
 milk
14-oz. can cream of coconut
1 t. vanilla extract

1 c. white rum, or 1/2 c. white
 rum plus 1/2 c. water,
 or 1 c. water
1/4 t. ground cloves
1/2 t. cinnamon

In the top of a double boiler, combine egg yolks and evaporated milk. Mix well. Stirring constantly, cook over lightly simmering water until mixture reaches 160 degrees on a candy thermometer and is thick enough to coat the back of a spoon. Transfer mixture to a blender; add remaining ingredients. Blend for at least 30 seconds. Pour into glass bottles; cover and chill overnight. Before serving, give bottles a good shake to make sure all the spices and coconut are mixed well. Makes 20 servings.

Nestle a punch bowl in an evergreen wreath...tuck in fresh red carnations on picks as an accent. So pretty and sweet-smelling too!

Christmas Cocoa

Shirl Parsons
Cape Carteret, NC

Perfect for the holiday season! Snuggle up by the fire with a steaming mug of gourmet hot chocolate. For variety, you can add cinnamon and nutmeg before adding the milk, or use peppermint extract in place of vanilla.

1/2 c. Dutch-processed baking
   cocoa
1/4 c. powdered sugar
1/2 c. half-and-half

4 c. milk
1 t. vanilla extract
Garnish: whipped cream,
   grated chocolate

Combine cocoa and sugar in a saucepan; whisk in half-and-half until smooth. Over low heat, whisk in milk and vanilla; bring to a simmer. Pour into mugs; top with whipped cream and grated chocolate. Makes 4 servings.

Make yourself a mug of hot cocoa, settle into a cozy corner and take time to do some of those things you've been meaning to... call old friends, sort through Mom's recipe box or read the latest holiday home magazine.

INDEX

Appetizers

Beverages

Breads

Breakfasts

Candies

INDEX

INDEX

Find Gooseberry Patch
wherever you are!

www.gooseberrypatch.com

Email

Call us toll-free at 1·800·854·6673

handknit mittens strings of popcorn

homemade candy

sugar cookies

letters to Santa

holly & mistletoe

 sparkly tinsel paper snowflakes

U.S. to Metric Recipe Equivalents

Volume Measurements

1/4 teaspoon	1 mL
1/2 teaspoon	2 mL
1 teaspoon	5 mL
1 tablespoon = 3 teaspoons	15 mL
2 tablespoons = 1 fluid ounce	30 mL
1/4 cup	60 mL
1/3 cup	75 mL
1/2 cup = 4 fluid ounces	125 mL
1 cup = 8 fluid ounces	250 mL
2 cups = 1 pint =16 fluid ounces	500 mL
4 cups = 1 quart	1 L

Weights

1 ounce	30 g
4 ounces	120 g
8 ounces	225 g
16 ounces = 1 pound	450 g

Oven Temperatures

300° F	150° C
325° F	160° C
350° F	180° C
375° F	190° C
400° F	200° C
450° F	230° C

Baking Pan Sizes

Square		Loaf	
8x8x2 inches	2 L = 20x20x5 cm	9x5x3 inches	2 L = 23x13x7 cm
9x9x2 inches	2.5 L = 23x23x5 cm	Round	
Rectangular		8x1-1/2 inches	1.2 L = 20x4 cm
13x9x2 inches	3.5 L = 33x23x5 cm	9x1-1/2 inches	1.5 L = 23x4 cm